美国语文

── ★ 和大自然做朋友 ★ ──

[美] 埃德温·埃尔德曼 ◎ 主编
帕孜丽娅·阿力木 等 ◎ 译

苏州新闻出版集团
古吴轩出版社

图书在版编目（CIP）数据

美国语文.和大自然做朋友/(美)埃德温·埃尔德曼主编；
帕孜丽娅·阿力木等译. -- 苏州：古吴轩出版社，2016.12（2024.9重印）
ISBN 978-7-5546-0787-9

Ⅰ.①美… Ⅱ.①埃…②帕… Ⅲ.①英语课—小学—美国—教材
Ⅳ.①G624.311

中国版本图书馆CIP数据核字(2016)第248043号

责任编辑：蒋丽华
见习编辑：薛　芳
策　　划：党霄羽
封面设计：沈加坤

书　　名：**美国语文——和大自然做朋友**
主　　编：[美]埃德温·埃尔德曼
译　　者：帕孜丽娅·阿力木　等
出版发行：苏州新闻出版集团
　　　　　古吴轩出版社
　　　　　地址：苏州市八达街118号苏州新闻大厦30F
　　　　　电话：0512-65233679　　邮编：215123
出 版 人：王乐飞
印　　刷：天津旭非印刷有限公司
开　　本：690mm×980mm　1/16
印　　张：12.75
版　　次：2016年12月第1版
印　　次：2024年9月第2次印刷
书　　号：ISBN 978-7-5546-0787-9
定　　价：49.80元

如有印装质量问题，请与印刷厂联系：022-22520876

推荐序一

李江月

（伊利诺斯大学PHD，湖北省高考作文满分获得者）

  我在美国留学的时候，不仅要承担繁重的学习任务，还要传道授业，帮自己的导师们带本科新生。那时候我就经常想，要是有一套全新的教材，难度适中，学生和教师都能在书中获得营养，让来自中国的学生既能学习原汁原味的地道的美式英语，又能对自己所学的专业有所帮助，还能和各个领域的大咖们谈笑风生，打破很多美国人觉得中国人就是书呆子的刻板印象，那该多好啊！

  这部千呼万唤始出来的《美国语文》丛书，解决了大家英语学习和教学的需求。每一篇课文都有精美的翻译，译文都做到了信达雅，读起来让人感觉如沐春风，甚至有时候让人感动，让学习英语这个看上去很繁重很枯燥的历程充满了惊喜。

  众所周知，英语是不断变化的语言，也许需要每个学习者终身不断地学习。本套书的英文原版，是由常青藤名校校长精编精选，汇集了许多名家的经典之作，所以我们每一位读者，不仅是学生，还包括老师和家长，都能在这样美妙的阅读中感受到自己的进步，得到切切实实的满足感。这些美丽的体验，是市面上一般读物难以给予我们的。

相比很多所谓"高屋建瓴"的语言学著作，这部丛书经历了实践的考验，是一部非常亲民和接地气的青少年读物，也是家长和老师很好的帮手。

很多时候，因为应试教育的需求，同学们不得不死记硬背许多文学大家的作品，但是他们并不理解这些作品。于是，虽然短期内成绩提高了，却在成年后丧失了对文学的爱好和学习的欲望。不论在中国还是美国，总能看到这样令人遗憾的现象。对此，我们觉得很可惜，学习文学本来应该是一种乐趣，而不应该是一种负担。我们希望孩子们开心地学，家长们愉快地陪伴他们学习，老师们欣喜地发现孩子们的进步，而不是扼杀他们的兴趣，阻碍他们进一步追求知识的脚步。

我们知道，很多文学大师虽然不是专门的儿童作家，但是他们并不是没有给孩子写过作品。本套书的一大亮点就是集结了很多大家笔下从未被翻译成汉语的遗珠之作——在各领域专门为孩子创作的作品。通过阅读本套书，孩子们能在书中了解到许多新奇的知识，坐在家里就环游世界，也为未来的学习打下扎实的基础。

本书主编埃德温·埃尔德曼先生，用他的智慧和孜孜不倦的努力，代替了我们在文山书海的盲目搜寻，就像我们的另一双眼睛，带我们遨游浩瀚的书海，获取人类文明的精华。

一言以蔽之，这套丛书是我用过的最好的美国语文学习、教学的教材，既可以用来自学，也可以用到课堂上。特此，我将这部丛书诚挚推荐给大家。让我们一起在《美国语文》的海洋里自由地冲浪吧！

推荐序二

曹海元
（MIT PHD）

迄今为止，阅读一直是我最大的爱好，而在现今残存的记忆里，我最早读到可以真正称得上书的，正是父亲给我的那套页面泛黄的《上下五千年》。我在脑海里至今仍旧清晰地记得那套书的封面，茕茕孑立的烽火台，赭红的城楼，残阳如血。华夏五千年那时而诡谲绵密时而波澜壮阔的历史也随着作者娓娓道来的小故事，奔涌到我充满好奇的内心，溅起了一片片波澜。虽然以我当时的阅历和见识无法理解许多深奥的名词和藏在历史故事背后深刻的道理，但是那套书唤起了我内心对于知识的渴望。阅读让我得以坐上时光机，身临其境般在华夏文明的浩瀚长河中自由穿梭，在我的心中种下了星星之火。正是这些星星点点的火种，照亮了我内心通往知识殿堂的道路，让阅读成了我生命中最大的乐趣，从而造就了我今天这副模样。

《上下五千年》那套书在我如今看来，也许简陋不堪，只是一些历史小故事汇编，但在当年那个懵懂少年看来却已然是通往圣杯的指路明灯。如今这套《美国语文》无论从文章的文学艺术性、选材的宽泛多样性来说，还是从编排的科学合理性上来看，都要遥遥领先。阅读这套书的少年从中可以先领略中世纪灿若星河的文艺复兴，再遇见近现代疾风怒涛般的工业革命；可以先认识一生锋芒毕露最后却功亏一篑的拿破仑，再偶遇始终沉默寡言却在危难之际挽大厦于将倾的华盛顿。从弗吉尼亚的崎岖山岭到欧亚大陆的广袤平原，短短千言却包罗万象、荟萃乾坤，包含了世界历史、地理、博物、人物、传奇、诗歌等领域的精华。

在我看来，如果说《上下五千年》只是星星点点的火苗，那么这套《美国语文》则是那光芒四射的火炬。我想读者尤其是那些处于学习阶段的青少年，必然可以像当年的我那样，从这套书中找到点燃自己心中火种的火焰，照亮通往圣杯的道路。

最后，用我最爱的诗歌《伊萨卡岛》中的一句话来结尾——"当你启程，前往伊萨卡岛时，愿你的道路漫长，充满奇迹，充满发现。"这也是我对所有有幸读到这套丛书的读者的祝福。我想说的就这么多了，希望我无知和浅薄的序言不会让这套书的光芒逊色。

Preface

This book is designed to be the first placed in the child's hands when he enters school. It is carefully arranged so that it can be used with equal success by all teachers, whether they adopt the sentence method, the word method, or the phonic method. In this way it is equally well adapted to graded schools where the entire time of the teacher is devoted to the class studying it, and to upgraded schools where one teacher must do all the work of six or more grades.

Every lesson is a simple, closely connected story, and in itself makes complete sense. For the first thirty-eight pages these stories have been prepared for this book; from that point on, every one, except review lessons, is a recognized classic for children. All educational authorities agree that this is desirable.

The words used are selected from the home vocabulary of the child, and no word is ever used in the reading exercise unless it has been first placed in the list at the head of the lesson.

At frequent intervals through the book review lessons are given in which words previously learned are presented in new combinations.

The illustrations in black and white are simple pictures which suggest only the thought involved in the lesson they illustrate, thus conforming to modern pedagogical views on this point.

Our thanks are due to Messrs. Houghton, Mifflin & Co. for permission to use the poem "The Little Bird," by Joel Chandler Harris.

前 言

　　本书是学龄儿童的首选读物。书中的内容经过精心安排,所以无论教师们是否采用书中的句式、单词或发音的学习方法,都能用本书在教学上取得同样的成效。因此,本书既适用于分年级教学的学校,也适用于跨年级教学的学校。

　　本书通俗易懂,每一课的故事之间都有密切的联系,而且每一课也都是一个完整的故事。前三十八页的故事是在为后面的部分准备,从第三十九页开始,除了复习课以外,所有的故事都是公认的儿童读物的经典。教育界的权威们一致认为,本书值得一读。

　　本书里的单词均是孩子们在家庭中已经学到的,除了每课前面词汇表里的单词外,每一课都没有生词。

　　阅读篇目中还穿插着复习课。复习课的内容是用前几课中出现的生词写成的新故事。

　　本书插图均为黑白简笔画,主要用途是帮助读者理解文章中的内容观点,这也是当代教学法的体现。

　　感谢霍顿先生和米夫林先生允许我们收录乔尔·钱德勒·哈里斯的诗歌《小鸟》。

目 录

Chapter 1 | 第一章 001

Lesson 1..003
Lesson 2..004
Lesson 3..005
Lesson 4..006
Lesson 5..008
Lesson 6　Review..................................010

Chapter 2 | 第二章 013

Lesson 7..015
Lesson 8..016
Lesson 9..017
Lesson 10..019
Lesson 11..021
Lesson 12..023
Lesson 13..025
Lesson 14..027
Lesson 15..029
Lesson 16..031
Lesson 17　Review................................033

Chapter 3 | 第三章 035

Lesson 18..037
Lesson 19..039
Lesson 20..041
Lesson 21..043
Lesson 22..045
Lesson 23..047
Lesson 24..048
Lesson 25..050
Lesson 26..054
Lesson 27　Review..055

Chapter 4 | 第四章 057

Lesson 28..059
Lesson 29..061
Lesson 30..062
Lesson 31..064
Lesson 32..065
Lesson 33..066
Lesson 34..067
Lesson 35..069
Lesson 36..071
Lesson 37..073

Lesson 38..074

Lesson 39..076

Lesson 40..077

Lesson 41..078

Lesson 42..082

Lesson 43..083

Lesson 44..085

Lesson 45..087

Lesson 46..088

Lesson 47..090

Lesson 48..091

Lesson 49..092

Lesson 50..094

Lesson 51..096

Lesson 52　Review..098

Chapter 5 | 第五章 101

Lesson 53..103

Lesson 54..105

Lesson 55..107

Lesson 56..109

Lesson 57..110

Lesson 58..111

Lesson 59..113

Lesson 60 114
Lesson 61 116
Lesson 62 118
Lesson 63 120
Lesson 64　Review 121

Chapter 6 | 第六章 123

Lesson 65 125
Lesson 66 127
Lesson 67 129
Lesson 68 131
Lesson 69 132
Lesson 70 134
Lesson 71 136
Lesson 72 137
Lesson 73 139
Lesson 74 141
Lesson 75　Review 143

Chapter 7 | 第七章 145

Lesson 76 147
Lesson 77 149
Lesson 78 151

Lesson 79 152
Lesson 80 156
Lesson 81 158
Lesson 82 160
Lesson 83 163
Lesson 84 166
Lesson 85 168
Lesson 86 169
Lesson 87 172
Lesson 88 173
Lesson 89 174
Lesson 90 177
Lesson 91 181
Lesson 92 186
Lesson 93 187
Lesson 94 188

Chapter 1 | 第一章

Lesson 1

The boy is Ned.
Ned is a boy.
The boy has a dog.
The boy is Ned.
Ned has a dog.
The dog is Bob.

🖋 译文

这个男孩是耐德。
耐德是个小男孩。
这个男孩有条狗。
男孩名字叫耐德。
男孩耐德有条狗。
小狗名字叫鲍勃。

Lesson 2

A dog has a cap.
The cap is on the dog.
The dog is Bob.
Bob has a cap.

The cap is on a box.
Ned can get the cap.
Bob, get the cap.
Get the cap, Ned.

译文

一条狗儿有顶帽。
帽子戴在小狗头。
这条小狗是鲍勃。
鲍勃有顶帽子喔。

帽子在那箱子上。
耐德能够够得着。
鲍勃,快去拿帽子。
耐德得到了那顶帽。

Lesson 3

The girl is Nan.
Nan has a cat.
The boy has a dog.
The girl has a cat.

The cat is Tab.
Tab has a bed.
The bed is in the box.
Tab is in the bed.

译文

这个女孩名叫楠。
楠有一只小猫咪。
那个男孩有条狗。
这个女孩有只猫。

这只猫咪叫泰布。
猫咪泰布有张床。
床在那个盒子里。
泰布在那张床上。

Lesson 4

Nan has a hen.
The hen has a nest.
The nest is in a box.
The hen is on the nest.
Nan fed the hen.
Can Bob get the hen?

Ned has a top.
Ned can spin the top.
The top can hum.
Spin the top, Ned.

Can Nan spin a top?
A girl can spin a top.
Spin the top, Nan.

译文

楠有一只小母鸡。
这只母鸡有个窝。
窝在一个盒子里。
母鸡就在那窝里。
楠喂过了母鸡。
鲍勃能不能抓住这母鸡?

耐德有一个陀螺。
耐德会抽陀螺哦。
陀螺发出"嗡嗡"声。
耐德快来抽陀螺。

女孩楠会抽陀螺吗?
一个女孩会抽陀螺。
楠,快来抽陀螺。

Lesson 5

A cat is on the box.
The cat is not Tab.
A jug is on the box.
Milk is in the jug.
The cat cannot get the milk.
The girl has not fed the cat.

A man has a dog.
The dog is not Bob.
A boy fed the dog.
The dog can run.
The man has a gun.
The man and the dog can run.

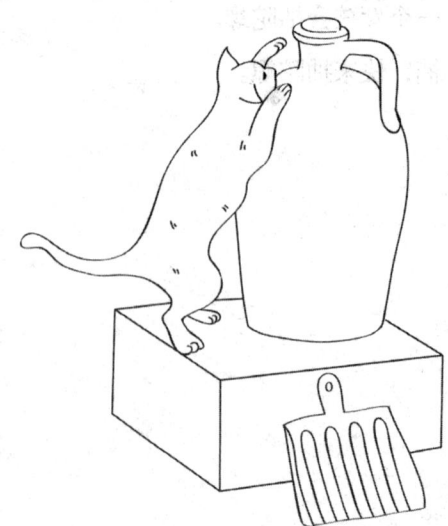

译义

有只猫咪在盒上。
这只猫咪不是泰布。
一个罐子在盒上。
牛奶在那罐子中。
猫咪喝不到牛奶。
女孩还没喂猫咪。

有个男人有条狗。
那条狗不是鲍勃。
有个男孩喂了狗。
这条小狗很会跑。
那个男人有支枪。
男人和狗都会跑。

Lesson 6 Review

The girl has milk in the jug.
The girl is Nan.
Nan has fed Tab and the dog.
Nan has not fed the hen.
The hen is on the nest.
Ned and Bob run.
Ned has a top.
Bob has a cap.
Ned can spin the top.
Bob can not spin the top.
The top can hum.

The cat has a bed in the box.
The dog is in the bed.
A gun is on the box.
The boy can not get the gun.
The man can get the gun.

✏ 译文（复习课）

女孩的牛奶在罐子里。
这个女孩就是楠。
楠喂了泰布和那条狗。
楠还没有喂母鸡。
母鸡还在那窝里。
耐德和鲍勃在跑步。
耐德有一个陀螺。
鲍勃有一顶帽子。
耐德会打陀螺。
鲍勃不会打陀螺。
陀螺转起来，"嗡嗡嗡"。

猫有一张在盒子里的床。
狗正趴在那床上。
盒子上，有把枪。
男孩拿不到那把枪。
男人可以拿到那把枪。

Chapter 2 | 第二章

Lesson 7

🔖 预习

flag /flæg/ 旗子 **one** /wʌn/ 一个
here /hɪə/ 这里

Here is one flag.
Here are two flags.
One flag and one flag are two flags.

🔖 译文

这里有一面旗。
这里有两面旗。
一面旗加一面旗等于两面旗。

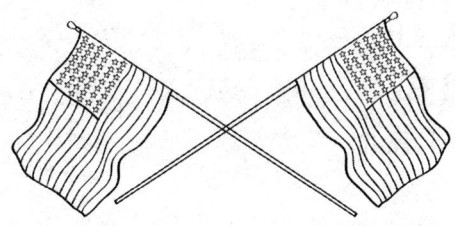

Lesson 8

☞ 预习

hat /hæt/ 帽子　　**my** /maɪ/ 我的
white /waɪt/ 白色的　　**black** /blæk/ 黑色的

Nan has a hat.
The hat is white.
The hat is on a box.
Tab is on the hat.
My hat is black.

☞ 译文

楠有一顶帽子。
这顶帽子是白的。
帽子在盒子上。
泰布在帽子上。
我的帽子是黑的。

Lesson 9

🖉 预习

me /mi:/ 我（宾格）　　　**let** /let/ 允许

My top is white.
Ned has a black top.
I let Ned spin my top.
Ned let me spin his top.
The black top is on the box.
The top can spin and hum.
My top is not on the box.
The white top can hum.
My top can spin on a box.

🖋 译文

我的陀螺是白的。
耐德的陀螺是黑的。
我把陀螺给耐德玩。
耐德把陀螺给我玩。
黑色的陀螺在盒子上。
陀螺能转还会"嗡嗡"响。
我的陀螺不在盒子上。
白色的陀螺也会"嗡嗡"响。
我的陀螺也能在盒子上转。

Lesson 10

☆ 预习

see /si:/ 看见 **sing** /sɪŋ/ 唱歌
robin /ˈrɒbɪn/ 知更鸟

I can see a robin.
The robin can sing.
The robin has a nest.
The robin is not on the nest.

This robin has an egg.
The egg is in the nest.
I can not see the egg.

The robin can hop.
The robin can sing.
I can hop, and I can sing.
But I am not a robin.

译文

我看到了一只知更鸟。
知更鸟的歌儿唱得好。
知更鸟还有一个窝。
知更鸟不在那窝里面。

知更鸟生了一只蛋。
蛋就在那窝里面。
那只蛋我看不见。

知更鸟会齐足跳。
知更鸟还会唱歌。
我会齐足跳,我也会唱歌。
但我不是一只知更鸟。

Lesson 11

✏ 预习

tree /tri:/ 树 *three* /θri:/ 三
four /fɔ:/ 四

One tree and two trees are three trees.
Two trees and two trees are four trees.
One tree and three trees are four trees.

One,two,three,four.

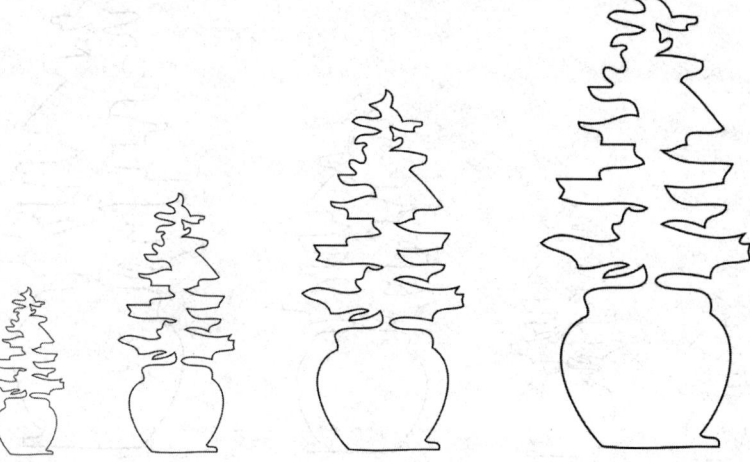

译文

一棵树加两棵树等于三棵树。
两棵树加两棵树等于四棵树。
一棵树加三棵树等于四棵树。

一，二，三，四。

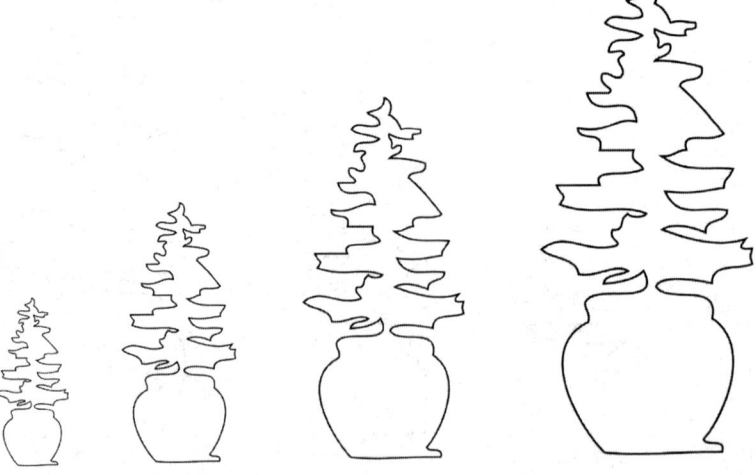

Lesson 12

✎ 预习

pet /pet/　宠物　　　　**lap** /læp/　膝盖
Tip /tɪp/　（狗名）提普

Kate has a pet dog.
The dog is in Kate's lap.
"Let me see the dog, Kate."
This is the pet dog.
This dog is Tip.
The pet dog has a bed.
Tip is Kate's pet dog.
The dog can sit up.
He can sit up and beg.
"Sit up, Tip, and beg."

I can see the dog beg.
My dog can sit up.
He can sit in my lap.
But he can not beg.

译文

凯特有条宠物狗。
小狗坐在凯特腿上。
"凯特,让我看看你的狗。"
这是那条宠物狗。
小狗名字叫提普。
宠物小狗有张床。
提普是凯特的宠物狗。
宠物提普会坐起来。
他会坐起来也会讨吃的。
"坐下来,提普,来讨吃的。"

我看到小狗在讨食。
我的狗会坐起来。
他会静静坐在我腿上。
但他不会讨吃的。

Lesson 13

预习

it /ɪt/ 它
rag /ræg/ 破布
wax /waks/ 蜡
doll /dɒl/ 娃娃

This is my big box.
My doll is in the box.
It is my doll's bed.
My dog is a rag doll.

Kate has a wax doll.
It is in Kate's bed.
I see the wax doll.

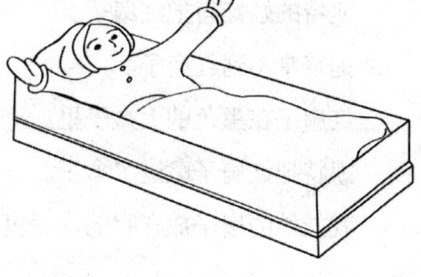

My doll has a fan.
The fan is white.
Kate's doll has a red fan.
Tip can not get the red fan.
It is in a big black box.
Kate hid the red fan in a box.
My doll's fan is in my box.

译文

这是我的大盒子。
盒子里有我的洋娃娃。
盒子是洋娃娃的床。
我的狗其实是个布娃娃。

凯特有一个蜡娃娃。
那个娃娃在凯特床上。
我看到了蜡娃娃。

我的娃娃有把扇子。
这把扇子是白的。
凯特的娃娃有把红扇子。
提普拿不到红扇子。
红扇子在黑色的大盒子里。
凯特把红扇子藏进了盒子。
我娃娃的扇子放在我的盒子里。

Lesson 14

✎ 预习

rug /rʌg/ 毯子   *she* /ʃiː/ 她
had /hæd/ 有   *nap* /næp/ 瞌睡

Tab is on the rug.
She has had a nap.
She is Nan's pet cat.
Tab is black and white.
Tab is not a big cat.

The rat hid in a box.
Tab did not see the rat.
Nan had a nut in the box.
The rat got the nut.
But the cat did not get the rat.
Nan sees the cat.
She can not see the nut.
Did Tab get the nut?

译文

泰布躺在毯子上。
她已经打了一会儿盹。
她是楠的宠物猫。
泰布是黑白色的小花猫。
她的个头可不大。

有只老鼠藏在了盒子里,
泰布没有看到这只老鼠。
楠的坚果放在了盒子里。
老鼠吃了坚果,
但没有被抓住。
楠看到了猫咪,
但没有看到坚果。
"是泰布吃掉了坚果吗?"

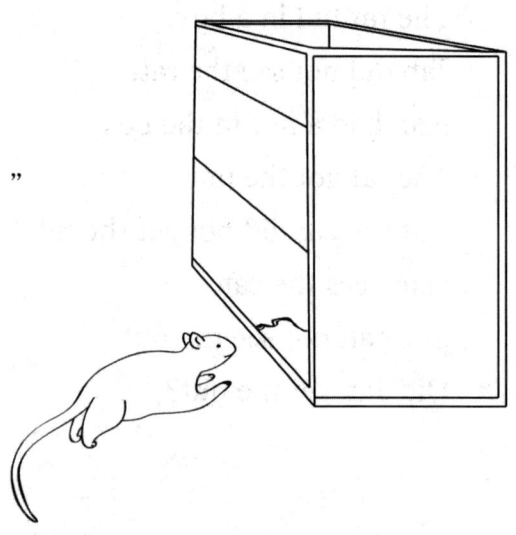

Lesson 15

✎ 预习

    dig /dɪg/ 挖   ***sand*** /sænd/ 沙子
    well /wel/ 井   ***tub*** /tʌb/ 桶

My doll is on the sand.
She can see me dig.
I dig in the sand.
The sand is soft and white.
It is in the big tub.
I can dig a well.
This well is a doll's well.

See Hal march.
Hal has his drum in his hand.
I can see the top of the drum.
The top of the drum is white.
Hal's gun is on the box.
Hal has a flag.
The flag is in his cap.

译文

我的洋娃娃,坐在沙子上。
我在挖呀挖,她在一旁看。
我在挖沙子。
沙子白又软,
装在大桶里。
我能挖出一个井,
送给我的洋娃娃。

看,哈尔在大步向前走。
手上拿着一面鼓。
我能看到那鼓面,
鼓面颜色是白的。
哈尔的枪在盒子上。
哈尔有一面旗。
旗插在他的帽子上。

Lesson 16

✏ **预习**

back /bæk/ 后背　　　　**will** /wɪl/ 将要
Billy /bɪli/ （人名）比利

This horse is Billy.
Billy is Rob's horse.
Rob can get up on Billy's back.
The horse will not run.
Billy is a big horse.
He will let Rob get up.
Rob is a big boy.

This pony is Dan.
Dan is my pony.
He is not big.
I can get up on Dan.
I met Rob.
Rob had his horse.
I had my pony.

译文

这匹马叫比利。
比利是罗布的马。
罗布能骑到马背上。
这匹马不会跑。
比利是一匹大马。
他会让罗布骑到他背上。
罗布是一个大男孩。

这匹小马叫丹。
丹是我的小马。
他个头不大。
我可以骑到他背上。
我遇见了罗布。
他有他的大马。
我有我的小马。

Lesson 17   Review

This is a robin, Kate. It can sing.
It has a nest and four eggs.
The robin can hop on the sand.
It will not sit on my hand.

A girl had a big wax doll.
The doll had a nap in a soft bed.
She had a red and black cap.

Tip is my pet dog.
He hid the doll's cap in his rug.
"Let me get up on the horse, Rob."
"Get up, Hal."
I will not let Billy run.
Three boys are on the back of my horse.

✍ 译文（复习课）

这是一只知更鸟，名字叫凯特。凯特会唱歌。
它有一个窝，生了四只蛋。
这只知更鸟，会在沙滩上跳呀跳。
但它不会坐在我手上。

一个小女孩，她有一个大大的蜡娃娃。
蜡娃娃，在软软的床上打着盹，
她有一顶红黑相间的花帽子。

提普是我的宠物狗，
他把蜡娃娃的帽子藏在了毯子里。
"让我骑到马上吧，罗布。"
"骑上来，哈尔。"
我不会让比利跑掉的。
三个男孩骑到了我的马背上。

Chapter 3 | 第三章

Lesson 18

✎ 预习

duck /dʌk/ 鸭子   **fox** /fɒks/ 狐狸
pond /pɑ:nd/ 池塘   **swim** /swɪm/ 游泳

The duck is on the pond.
She can swim and dive.
A hen can not swim and dive.
The fox can see the duck.
But he can not swim.
He can not get the duck.
This duck has a nest.
The fox can not see the nest.
The duck hid it.
Eggs are in the nest.
The fox can not get the eggs.
The duck will sit on the eggs.

译文

池塘里有一只鸭子,
她会游泳也会潜水。
有一只母鸡,
她不会游泳,也不会潜水。
狐狸看着这只鸭子,
但他不会游泳。
所以他没办法捉到鸭子。
鸭子有个窝。
狐狸看不到这个窝。
鸭子把窝藏起来了。
窝里有她下的蛋。
狐狸得不到鸭蛋。
鸭子会坐在蛋上孵鸭蛋。

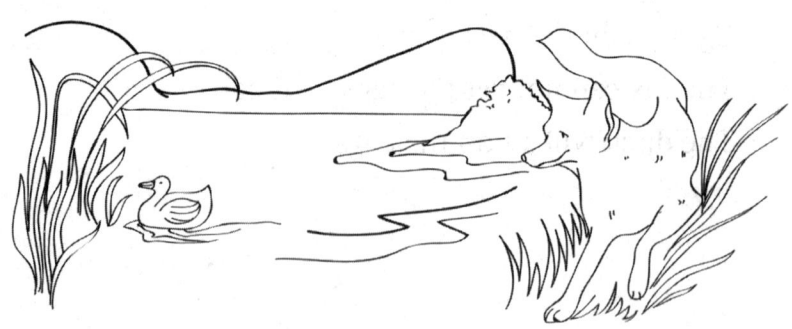

Lesson 19

📖 预习

Tom /tɒm/ （人名）汤姆　　***toy*** /tɔɪ/ 玩具
set /set/ 一套　　　　　　***shop*** /ʃɒp/ 工作室

Tom has a shop.
His shop is a big box.
He has a set of tools.
Tom can make a top.
Can he make a gun?
Tom can make a toy gun.

Tom gave Kate a top.
The top is made of a spool.
Tom made Kate's top.
He made the black peg, too.
Tom's top is made of tin.
He did not make this top.

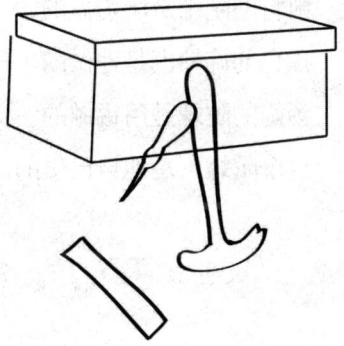

译文

汤姆有一个工作室。
他的工作室是一个大盒子。
汤姆有一套工具。
他会做陀螺。
他会做手枪吗?
汤姆会做玩具枪。

汤姆给了凯特一个陀螺,
那是一个用线轴做的陀螺。
凯特的陀螺是汤姆做的,
黑色的旋轴也是他做的。
汤姆的陀螺是用锡做的。
这个陀螺不是他自己做的。

Lesson 20

✎ 预习

five /faɪv/ 五 *six* /sɪks/ 六
seven /ˈsevn/ 七 *eight* /eɪt/ 八
nine /naɪn/ 九 *ten* /ten/ 十

Two birds and three birds are five birds.
One bird and four birds are five birds.
I see four blue birds.
I see four black birds.
I see two red birds.
I can count to six.
I can count to seven.

译文

两只鸟加三只鸟等于五只鸟。
一只鸟加四只鸟等于五只鸟。
我看见了四只蓝色的鸟。
我看见了四只黑色的鸟。
我看见了两只红色的鸟。
我能数到六。
我能数到七。

Lesson 21

This is Tom's room.
He and Kate play in this room.
Tom has Kate's hoop.
He did not make the hoop.
But he made a box.
Tom's toys are in the box.
Tip can not get the toys.
He will play with Tom and Kate.
Tom and Kate like to play with Tip.
Jack can count to ten.
I can, too. It is not hard.
I like to count.

译文

这是汤姆的房间。
他和凯特在房间里玩。
汤姆拿着凯特的铁环,
这个铁环不是他做的。
但他做了一个箱子。
汤姆把玩具放在了这个箱子里。
提普拿不到那些玩具,
他会和汤姆还有凯特一起玩。
汤姆与凯特喜欢和提普一起玩。
杰克能数到十。
我也会,这并不难。
我喜欢数数。

Lesson 22

Roy is at play with his dog.
He and the dog are on the hay.
Roy has a gun and a bag.
He will hunt a fox.
Roy plays that a fox is in the hay.

The name of Roy's dog is Dash.
Roy and Dash like to play.
Roy hid his cap in the hay.
Dash ran to hunt the cap.
Now he is back.
"Bow-wow! This is the cap."
How did Dash get the cap?

译文

罗伊在和他的小狗一起玩。
他和他的狗在干草丛上玩耍。
罗伊带着一支枪和一只包,
他准备去猎一只狐狸,
假装那只狐狸就在干草里。

罗伊的狗名字叫达什。
罗伊和达什都喜欢做游戏。
罗伊把他的帽子藏在干草里,
达什跑去找那顶帽子。
现在他跑回来了,
"汪汪汪,这是帽子。"
达什是怎么找到帽子的?

Lesson 23

"One, two, three, four, five, six, seven, eight, nine, ten," counts Jack, "Ready! Here I come."

Nan hides. "Whoop!" she calls.

Now Jack will seek Nan.

Jack and Nan like to play hide and seek. It is a fine game.

译文

"一,二,三,四,五,六,七,八,九,十。"杰克数着数,"准备好了吗?我来啦!"

楠藏了起来。"喂!"她叫道。

现在杰克要去找楠。

杰克和楠喜欢捉迷藏,这是一个很开心的游戏。

Lesson 24

Roy's hens are in the barn.
He has ten hens.
Roy fed the hens.
A rat came to the barn.
He came to take the food of the hens.
Dash made the rat run to his hole.

Roy and Dash will hunt the eggs,
Dash can help Roy in this way.
The dog is up on the hay.
Now he barks, "Bow-wow."
That is to say, "I see a nest.
But Roy may get the eggs."
Then Roy will get the eggs.

译文

罗伊的母鸡都在谷仓里,
他有十只母鸡。
罗伊喂完这些母鸡,
一只老鼠溜到了谷仓里。
他来和母鸡们抢食。
达什把老鼠赶回了洞里。

罗伊和达什一起去找鸡蛋,
达什能够帮罗伊。
达什站到了干草上,
现在他开始叫:"汪汪汪!"
他意思是:"我看到鸡窝了。
这样罗伊就能拿到鸡蛋了。"
于是,罗伊就可以拿到鸡蛋了。

Lesson 25

Ned has made a kite.
How big and strong it is!
The kite has a long tail.
This tail will help the kite to fly.
The kite is white.
The tail is red and white.
The name of the kite is Red Star.

Tom came to play with Ned.
Then the boys went to the hill.
Ned had his kite.

Tom had a long string.

He gave this string to Ned to fly the kite.

Soon the boys made the kite fly.

Ned held the string in his hand.

Tom held the kite.
Then Ned ran.
Up went the kite.

The wind made the kite go far, far up.

By and by the kite was far up in the sky.

The wind held it up well.

Then Tom went to help a small boy.

This boy's kite did not fly well.

It fell into a tall tree.

Tom had to climb the tree.

But he soon had the boy's kite.

译文

耐德做了一只风筝。
风筝又大又结实!
风筝有一条长尾巴。
风筝尾巴能帮助风筝飞起来。
这只风筝是白色的。
风筝尾巴则是红白相间的。
风筝的名字叫红星。

汤姆来找耐德一起玩。
于是两个男孩走到小山边。
耐德拿着他的风筝。
汤姆拿着长长的线。
为把风筝放上天,汤姆把线给耐德。

两个男孩很快就把风筝放上了天。
耐德手里抓着线,
汤姆抓着那风筝。
然后耐德跑起来,
风筝一下飞上去。
风把风筝吹得远,风把风筝吹得高,
风筝不久就高飞到天空。
风筝在风中稳稳飞。

这时，汤姆跑去帮助一个小男孩。
这个小男孩的风筝没放好，
风筝飞进了大树里。
汤姆不得不爬上那棵树。
不过，很快他就拿到了小男孩的风筝。

Lesson 26

White sheep, white sheep,
On a blue hill.
When the wind stops,
You all stand still.

When the wind blows,
You walk away slow.
White sheep, white sheep,
Where do you go?

(Answer: Cloud)

译文

小白羊，小白羊，
在那蓝色小山上。
当那风儿不再吹，
你就静静站在山冈上。

当那风儿吹起时，
你就慢慢走远方。
小白羊，小白羊，
你要去何方？

（谜底：云朵）

Lesson 27 Review

The boys like to play in the barn. Roy and Ned will make a big hill of the soft hay.

Hal is too small to climb to the top of this hill. But Tom is tall and strong, and will help Hal.

Tom let Roy and Ned make a kite with his tools. The tools are in a room in the barn. Kate gave Roy a spool with a long string on it to fly the kite. She got the spool at a shop.

Now the boys march to the pond. Hal has his drum. "One, two, three, four!" he plays.

Roy will take his dog Dash to the pond. The dog will not bark at the ducks. The boys can not swim, but Dash can swim and dive.

译文（复习课）

男孩们想到谷仓里玩。罗伊和耐德会用软软的干草堆成一个大大的干草堆。

哈尔太小了，爬不到干草堆的顶上。但是汤姆又高又壮，他会帮助哈尔的。

汤姆把他的工具借给罗伊和耐德，让他们做了一个风筝。这些工具放在谷仓的一间小屋里。凯特给罗伊送了一个卷轴，卷轴上有长长的线，可以用来放风筝。卷轴是凯特在商店买来的。

现在男孩子们向池塘行进。哈尔拿着他的小手鼓，敲着："一，二，三，四！"

罗伊会带他的狗——达什，一起去池塘。达什不会冲着鸭子叫。男孩们不会游泳，但是达什会游泳也会潜水。

Chapter 4 | 第四章

Lesson 28

Max has a large ball.
He can play with this ball.
See the ball in his hands.
Now he will make it roll.
It will roll to the wall.
Then it will roll to Max.
Max can toss the ball in his hands.
Then he will toss the ball to Fred.
Fred will toss it back to Max.
"Get it, Max. Run and get the ball."
He has it. Now let's see how far Max can toss it.
He will make Fred run and get it, too.
This is the way Max and Fred play.

译文

马克斯有个很大的球。
他会去玩这个球。
看,他手中拿着球,
现在他要让球滚起来。
球会滚到墙角去,
接着又会滚回马克斯的身边来。
马克斯能将手中的球扔出去,
然后他会把球扔给弗雷德,
弗雷德再把球扔还给马克斯。
"去拿这个球,马克斯。快跑呀,去追上那个球。"
他追到球了。现在,让我们看看马克斯能把球扔多远吧。
他也会让弗雷德跑去拾球,
这是马克斯和弗雷德玩的一个游戏。

Lesson 29

Fred has a fine little cart.
He plays that his dog is a horse.
The dog can draw the cart.
He will take us to ride.
One day Fred and I went to ride.
By and by the dog saw a cat.
Then the dog ran, Fred and I fell out of the cart.

译文

弗雷德有辆精致的小推车。
他把他的狗当成马去拉小推车。
他的狗能拉动小推车。
他愿意带我们去乘车。
有一天，我和弗雷德去乘小推车。
不久，拉车的狗就看到了一只猫。
于是狗就跑起来，把我和弗雷德从车上甩了下来。

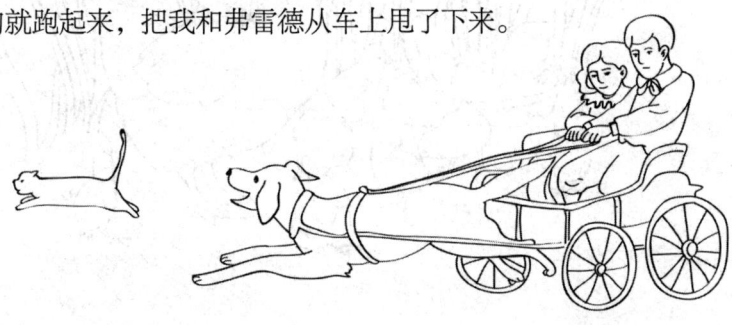

Lesson 30

This hen has ten chickens.
One chick is on the hen's back.
The chick will take a ride.
Will it not fall?
No! The chick can fly.
Fly down chick. You will fall.
"Peep, peep! I can not fall. I can fly."
The hen will say to her chick, "Cluck, cluck! Fly down!"

I saw you toss the kites on high,
And blow the birds about the sky.

译文

这只母鸡妈妈,带着十只小鸡。
有一只小鸡在鸡妈妈的背上。
它要坐在妈妈背上兜风去。
它不会摔下去吗?
不会!因为这只小鸡会飞。
飞得低一些啊,你会摔下去的。
"唧唧,唧唧!我不会摔下来,因为我会飞!"
而鸡妈妈会对她的孩子说,"咯咯,咯咯,快点飞下来!"

我看到你的风筝放得好高,
还撞到了空中飞翔的小鸟。

Lesson 31

I have a little sister,
Her name is peep, peep, peep.
She wades in the water,
Deep, deep, deep.
She climbs on the hilltop,
High, high, high.
Oh, oh, oh, my little sister,
Has but one eye.
What is she?

(Answer: Star, *Mother Goose*)

译文

我有一个小妹妹,
她的名字叫闪,闪,闪。
她游进了水里,
深,深,深。
她又爬上了山顶,
高,高,高。
哦,哦,哦,我的小妹妹,
她仅有一只眼睛。
她是什么?

(谜底:星星,《鹅妈妈》)

Lesson 32

As soft as silk,
As white as milk,
As bitter as gall,
A thick green wall, And a green coat covers me all.
What am I ?

(Answer:Walnut, *Mother Goose*)

✐ 译文

像丝绸一样的软,
像牛奶一样的白,
像胆汁一样的苦,
外面裹着厚厚的绿衣服。
我是什么?

(谜底:核桃,《鹅妈妈》)

Lesson 33

"My little girl has a cold, doctor. Can you make her well?"

"We will see. How did she get cold?"

"She went wading in the water."

"Will she take this? It is bitter."

"See how nicely she takes it, doctor."

"That is fine. She needs to take it three times a day. Then she will get well."

"医生,我的女儿感冒了。你能让她好起来吗?"

"让我们看看吧。她是怎么感冒的?"

"她去蹚水了。"

"她愿意吃这个药吗?这个药很苦。"

"她会乖乖吃下去的,医生。"

"那就好。这个药要一天吃三次。这样她就能好起来。"

Lesson 34

A little boy in the barn,
Lay down on some hay.
An owl came out,
And flew about.
And the little boy ran away.

(*Mother Goose*)

🔖 译文

谷仓里有一个小男孩，
躺在干草堆上。
一只猫头鹰飞来了，
在周围飞。
接着小男孩跑走了。

（《鹅妈妈》）

朗读

A boy's will is the wind's will.

(H.W. Longfellow)

少年的愿望就是风的愿望。

（亨利·沃兹沃斯·朗费罗）

Lesson 35

A fox went to take a walk. By and by he came to a well.

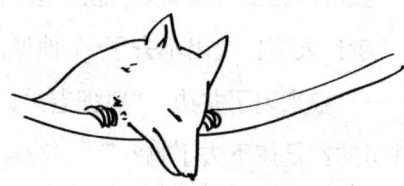

"I will climb up and peep in," he said. But the fox fell in.

"Oh, oh, I can not get out," he said.

A wolf came to the well. "Is that you, fox?" he said. "How did you get into the well? Did you fall in?"

"Can you climb out? Is the water deep? Poor fox! Will you have to stay in well?"

The fox did not like this. "Help me out, wolf," the fox said, "then you may take time to talk."

(*Aesop*, adapted)

译文

一只狐狸去散步。不一会儿,他就来到了一口井旁。

"我可以爬上去看看。"他说道。但狐狸却摔下去了。

"哦!天啊!我出不去了。"他说。

一只狼来到了井边。"狐狸老弟,是你吗?"狼问道。"你是怎么跑到井里的?是摔下去了吗?"

"你爬得出来吗?里面的水深吗?可怜的狐狸!你得一直待在井里吗?"

狐狸可不想一直待井里。"狼老兄,快帮我爬出去。"狐狸说,"有话你过会儿再说吧。"

(选自《伊索寓言》,有删改)

Lesson 36

May is Rob's little sister. Rob is good to her and likes to play with her.

One day a pet kid came to see Rob and May. Rob was glad to see him. May was not glad.

The kid ran up to Rob.

"How do you do, Dick?" Rob said.

Dick is the name of the kid.

"How big you are! By and by you will be a fine goat. Then you can draw my cart."

译文

梅是罗布的妹妹。罗布对妹妹特别好,也很喜欢和妹妹玩。

有一天,一只宠物山羊来看罗布和梅。罗布见了他很开心。但梅却不高兴。

小山羊朝罗布冲了过去。

"你怎么样啊?还好吗,迪克?"罗布说。

迪克是这只小山羊的名字。

"你真是长大了!看来再过不久你就能成为真正的山羊了。到那时候你就可以帮我拉小车了。"

Lesson 37

"Will you have some milk?" Then Rob held May's bottle out to Dick.

Dick drank a little of the milk. It was good. Then he drank and drank.

"Look at Dick. Is it not fun to see him, May?" Rob said.

But May did not like to see Dick take her milk.

"Do not cry, May," said Rob. "Let me feed poor Dick."

So Dick drank all the milk. Then he ran away, and was soon at home.

译文

"你想喝点牛奶吗？"罗布拿着梅的瓶子对迪克说道。

迪克尝了一小口牛奶。牛奶真好喝。于是，他就一直喝呀喝呀。

"你看迪克。梅，看看他，你不觉得有趣吗？"罗布说。

但梅不喜欢看迪克喝自己的牛奶。

"好啦，梅，别哭了。"罗布说，"让我好好喂喂这个可怜的小家伙。"

于是迪克就把牛奶全部喝光了。然后他就跑开了，很快就回了家。

Lesson 38

One day John and I went out to walk. We saw a tree on a high hill.

"Let us climb the hill," said John, "that tree has nuts on it."

Soon Max and his sister came by in a cart. The cart is large, and Max has two stout goats to pull it.

"Get into the cart," said Max, "and we will take you up the hill."

John got out at the top of the hill, and ran to the tree. He came back with one nut.

"It is like a hard green ball," he said.

He gave the nut to Max. "Oh, how bitter it is!" said Max. "Toss it away, John. Let us not stay to get nuts now."

We had a good time on the way home. The goats ran down the long hill.

译文

有一天,我和约翰一起出去散步。我们看到一座高山上有一棵树。

"我们去爬山吧,"约翰说,"山上有棵树,树上有坚果。"

不久,马克斯和他的妹妹坐着马车来了。这辆马车很大,由两只肥硕的山羊拉着它。

"上车吧,"马克斯说,"我们带你们上山。"

到了山顶,约翰从车上下来,朝那棵树跑了过去。然后,他带了一颗坚果回来了。

"它像一颗硬硬的绿色小球。"他说。

他把坚果给了马克斯。"哦!好苦呀!"马克斯说,"把它扔了吧,约翰。我们不要待在这里摘坚果了。"

回家的路上,我们玩得很开心。两只山羊从长长的山坡上跑了下去。

Lesson 39

A gray mouse met the white cat. The cat said, "Oh! Oh! I shall have a fine dinner."

Then gray mouse said, "Am I to have dinner with you? Just let me get my red silk coat. This gray coat is not nice."

The cat said, "You may get the coat. Please try not to stay away long."

So the mouse ran to his home in the wall. And the white cat did not get a mouse that day.

(Laurae Richards, adapted)

译文

一只灰鼠遇见了一只白猫。白猫说:"噢!噢!我要有一顿美味的晚餐了。"

这时灰鼠说:"你要我跟你共进晚餐吗?请先让我回去换上我那件红色的丝绸外套吧。灰色的这件不好看。"

猫说:"你可以去换外套。不过请不要耽搁太久哦。"

于是,那只灰鼠跑回了墙壁里的家。而白猫那天一只老鼠都没能吃到。

(劳罗·理查德,有删改)

Lesson 40

Little gray mouse, little gray mouse,
I beg you to stay in your fine little house;
If out here you come, to get just a crumb,
The cat will catch you as sure as you come.

译文

小灰鼠，小灰鼠，
你一定要乖乖待在自己精致的小屋；
如果你出来了，就为了一块面包屑，
只要你一来，那只猫就会把你抓住。

Lesson 41

Jane liked to play all the time.

One day her mother said, "You are now six years old, Jane. You must try to do some work." But Jane said, "I do not like to work. It is so hard. Please let me play today, Mother. Just this one day."

So Jane went to play in the woods.

By the brook, Jane met a gray squirrel.

"Oh, little squirrel! Come and play with me. You do not work, do you?"

"Yes, little girl. I have to hunt nuts for winter. I go to all the trees, and try to find the best." Then the squirrel ran away.

Soon a bee flew by. "Little bee, little bee, come and play with me. Do you work, little bee?"

"Yes, little girl. I must lay up honey for winter." Then the bee flew off.

Jane made a cup out a leaf. Then she had a nice drink. "I Work, I Work." the brook said.

Jane ran on. She met a little ant. "We Work." said the ant.

"We Work all day."

Then Jane sat down on a stone to think. "They all work," she said, "But they are happy. I must work." So she ran home. "They all work, Mother." she said, "The squirrel and the bee work. The brook and the ant work. What can I do?"

(German Classics)

译文

简总是喜欢玩。

有一天她妈妈对她说:"简,你现在六岁了。你必须得学着做点什么了。"但简回答说:"我不喜欢做事。做事真难啊。妈妈,今天就让我出去玩吧。就今天一天。"

于是简就去了树林玩。

在小溪边,简碰见了一只灰色的松鼠。

"哦,小松鼠!快来跟我玩吧。你不需要做事,对不对?"

"不是的,小姑娘。我必须储存坚果,才好过冬。我要爬遍所有的树,找到最好的一棵。"说完小松鼠就跑了。

过了一会儿,一只蜜蜂飞了过来。"小蜜蜂,小蜜蜂,快过来跟我玩吧。你要做事吗,小蜜蜂?"

"是啊,小姑娘。我必须储存蜂蜜,才好过冬。"然后蜜蜂就飞走了。

简用树叶泡了一杯茶,美美地喝着。"我在做事,我在做事。"小溪说道。

简继续向前跑去。这时,她碰到了一只小蚂蚁。"我们在做事。"蚂蚁说。

"我们整天都在做事。"

于是,简坐在一块石头上,陷入了沉思。"他们都在做事,"她说,"但他们很快乐。所以我也必须做事。"于是,她跑回了家。"妈妈,他们都在做事。"她说,"小松鼠和小蜜蜂在做事。小溪和蚂蚁也在做事。那我能做什么呢?"

(《德国经典故事》)

Lesson 42

Ding, dong, bell!
The cat is in the well.
Who put her in?
Little John Green.
Who will put her out?
Big John Stout.

(Mother Goose)

译文

叮咚叮咚,铃铛响!
小猫在那井里面。
是谁把她放进去的?
是小约翰·格林。
是谁把她放出来的?
是大约翰·斯图奥特。

(《鹅妈妈》)

Lesson 43

What does little birdie say,
In her nest at peep of day?
"Let me fly," says little birdie,
Mother, let me fly away."
What does little baby say?
In her bed at peep of day,
Baby says, like a little birdie,
"Let me rise and fly away."

(Alfred Tennyson)

译文

听,小鸟在说什么?
破晓时分她在她的鸟巢。
"让我飞吧,"小鸟在说,
"妈妈,让我飞走吧。"
"听,小宝宝在说什么?
破晓时分她躺在她的床上,
小宝宝说的和小鸟一样。
"让我快快起床,快点离开吧。"

(阿尔弗雷德·丁尼生)

> **思考**
>
> 小女孩子要怎么帮助妈妈呢?小男孩子又能做些什么事呢?

Lesson 44

One day a rabbit met a turtle. "Let us run a race," the rabbit said.

The turtle said, "That will be fine sport. Where shall we run?"

"Let us run to that old tree," the rabbit said. So they set out to run the race.

"The turtle is slow," the rabbit said. "I shall take a nap." So he went to sleep.

After some time he jumped up. He saw the turtle at the old tree.

"How did you get there so soon?" the rabbit said.

"I ran while you had a nap," the turtle said.

(Aesop, adapted)

译文

一天,一只兔子遇见了一只乌龟。"我们比赛跑步吧。"兔子对乌龟说。

乌龟说:"这可是个好运动。我们要跑到哪里呢?"

"我们就跑到那棵老树那里吧。"兔子说。于是,他们就开始比赛了。

"乌龟跑得真慢,"兔子抱怨道,"我都可以打会儿盹了。"于是,兔子就睡下了。

过了一会儿,兔子蹦了起来。他看见乌龟已经到了老树下。

"你怎么这么快就到了?"兔子问道。

"我只是把你睡觉的时间用来跑步罢了。"乌龟如是说。

(《伊索寓言》,有删改)

Lesson 45

The Cow

The friendly cow all red and white,
　I love with all my heart.
　She gives me cream with all her might,
　　To eat with apple tart.

(Robert Louis Stevenson)

🎧 译文

奶牛

红白色的小奶牛,
我最爱的小宝贝。
有了她的鲜奶油,
苹果馅饼才美味。

（罗伯特·路易斯·斯蒂芬逊）

Lesson 46

The Lion and the Mouse

The lion is the king of all the beasts. One day this lion lay down in the woods to take a nap.

In a little while a mouse ran over the lion's paw. This woke the lion. He was about to kill the mouse.

"Please, please do not kill me, King Lion," said the mouse. "Some day I may help you."

The lion laughed, but he let the mouse go. A big lion did not need the help of a mouse.

Not long after this the lion ran into a net. He worked and worked to get out, but the net was too strong.

The mouse came by. "I will help you, King Lion," he said. With his strong teeth, the mouse cut the net. Then the lion got out.

(Aesop, adapted)

✍ 译文

狮子与老鼠

狮子是万兽之王。有一天,狮子在树林里打盹。

过了一会儿,一只老鼠从狮子的爪子上偷偷溜过。这个小动作把狮子吵醒了。狮子大发雷霆,要杀死这只老鼠。

"求您,求您不要杀我,狮子大王。"老鼠恳求道,"或许哪一天我就能帮到您。"

听了这话,狮子大笑起来,但还是放老鼠走了。强大的狮子怎么会需要老鼠的帮助?

没过多久,这只狮子一不小心掉进了网里。为了逃出去,狮子使出了浑身解数,但网太牢固了。

那只老鼠恰好路过。"我会帮你的,狮子大王。"老鼠说。老鼠用锋利的牙齿咬呀咬呀,不一会儿,老鼠就咬断了网。于是,狮子就逃出来了。

(《伊索寓言》,有删改)

Lesson 47

Work while you work,
Play while you play;
That is the way,
To be happy and gay.

译文

工作时间就工作，
玩耍时间就玩耍；
只要做到这两点，
生活幸福又快乐。

Lesson 48

This is pumpkin vine. See what large flowers and leaves it has.

The flowers will turn into big yellow pumpkins. Pumpkins grow on thick stems, these hold the pumpkins to the vines.

What a strange-looking thing this is! It is a Jack-O-lantern. It is made out a pumpkin.

Boys like to make Jack-O-lanterns. They put candles in them to give light.

译文

这是南瓜的藤蔓。你看，它的花朵和叶片可真大呀！

这些花朵会慢慢长成黄色的大南瓜。南瓜结在粗壮的茎秆上，和藤蔓连在一起。

这个东西长得可真奇怪呀！它是南瓜灯。它是用南瓜做的。

男孩子们都很喜欢做南瓜灯。他们会把蜡烛放进里面，再把它点亮。

Lesson 49

The Six Sunbeams (1)

The sun had come up. He set out his warm beams.

One beam came to a little bird. The bird flew from its nest.

Then it sang, "Cheer up! Cheer up! Cheer up! Hear me sing! This is my song!"

One beam came to a little squirrel. "Jump up, little squirrel," it said. "Day has come, jump up."

Out came the squirrel from his hole in the oak tree. Then he ran away into the woods to find nuts.

(German Classics)

译文

六束阳光（1）

太阳出来了。他将温暖的光芒洒向大地。

一束光照在一只小鸟身上。小鸟从巢里飞了出来。

然后，它开始唱："起床啦！起床啦！起床啦！快来听我歌唱！这就是我的歌！"

一束光照在一只小松鼠身上。"快起来，小松鼠。"那束光说道，"天亮啦，新的一天开始了，起来啦。"

小松鼠从橡树上的洞穴里出来了。接着他就跑向了森林，他要去找坚果了。

（《德国经典故事》）

Lesson 50

The Six Sunbeams (2)

One beam came to the barn. There it saw the old roosters and the hens.

The little sunbeam woke the old rooster. He took his head from under his wing.

"It is time for me to crow," he said. "I must wake the hens."

Soon they all flew down. Then they went to hunt for food.

One beam came to a small house at the top of the barn. This was the home of the doves.

"Coo, coo!" they said. "Morning has come." So they flew away to find something to eat.

(German Classics)

译文

六束阳光（2）

一束光来到了谷仓之上。这里有一群老公鸡，还有一群母鸡。太阳光唤醒了一只老公鸡。他把脑袋从翅膀下抬了起来。

"又到我打鸣的时间了，"他说道，"我必须得把母鸡们叫起来。"

很快，他们都醒了过来。然后他们四散开去觅食了。

一束光照到了谷仓顶上的一间小屋上。这里是鸽子们的家。

"咕咕咕，咕咕咕！"他们说，"已经是早上了。"于是他们便飞走了，去找吃的了。

（《德国经典故事》）

Lesson 51

The Six Sunbeams (3)

One beam came to the beehive. And what did the bees do? They all came out, "Buzz, buzz, buzz!" Then they flew off to find the honey.

One beam came to the bed of a lazy boy. This boy liked to stay in bed in the morning.

"Get up, John, it is time to get up."

But John said, "Oh, I do not wish to get up. I wish to sleep."

So he turned over on his other side. Then he went to sleep again.

Did this little beam not feel sad?

(German Classics)

译文

六束阳光（3）

　　有一束光来到了蜂箱上。蜜蜂们在干什么呢？他们倾巢而出，"嗡嗡嗡，嗡嗡嗡，嗡嗡嗡！"地唱着。然后他们也飞走了，去找蜂蜜。

　　还有一束光来到了大懒虫床边，大懒虫是个小男孩。他早上特别喜欢赖床。

　　"起来啦，约翰，时间不早了，该起床了。"

　　但约翰说："哦，我一点都不想起来。我想睡觉。"

　　说完他便翻了个身，又睡着了。

　　这束光怎么会不难过呢？

（《德国经典故事》）

Lesson 52   Review

　　Grapes grow on vines. They have large green leaves. Some vines climb up into tepees. Others climb over high walls. Then the grapes can be seen.

　　I will tell you about a fox and some grapes. This fox had come out of the thick woods. He was looking for something to eat. After a while he saw some fine grapes on a high wall.

　　"How good these grapes look!" he said. "I must have some."

　　He was not a lazy fox, so he set to work to get them. He jumped up again and again. But the grapes grew too high for him. He did not get one grape.

　　"Oh, well! I do not wish to eat them," he said, "they are sour."

(Aesop, adapted)

✏ 译文（复习课）

　　藤蔓上满是葡萄。葡萄藤上有大片大片的绿叶。有一些藤蔓爬上了圆顶帐篷。另一些爬上了高高的墙。这样，我们也就能看到葡萄了。

　　下面，我要给你讲一个关于狐狸和葡萄的故事。这只狐狸从浓密的树林中出来。他在找吃的。不一会儿，他就发现，高墙上长着一些极好的葡萄。

　　"这些葡萄长得可真好啊！"他说，"我得摘点尝尝。"

　　他可不是懒狐狸，这不，他马上开始想办法摘葡萄了。他一次又一次地往上跳。可是葡萄长得太高了。他一颗葡萄都摘不到。

　　"哦，好吧！我一点都不想吃葡萄，"他说，"这些葡萄都是酸的呀。"

（《伊索寓言》，有删改）

Chapter 5 | 第五章

Lesson 53

"Stop, stop, pretty water,"
Said Mary one day,
To a bright little brook.
That was running away.

"You run on so fast!
I wish you would stay,
My boat and my flowers,
You will carry away."

"But I will run after,
Mother says that I may.
For I would know where,
You are running away."

(Eliza Lee Follen)

✎ 译文

"小溪，小溪，快停下。"
面对着清澈的小溪，
玛丽说道。
小溪却还是流走了。

"你跑得太快了！
我希望你能停下来，
这样我的小船与花朵，
你就能一起带走。"

"妈妈跟我说，
我可以追着你走；
但你要记得告诉我，
你在向哪儿流。"

（伊丽扎·里·福伦）

Lesson 54

The Little Boy's Coat (1)

A poor little boy had no coat. But he had to stay out in the cold to work. One day he met a little black lamb. The lamb said, "You need a coat. I will give you some wool from my back."

"Thank you," the boy said.

"Let me spin the wool," the spider said. "I can make a fine web." Soon the spider had made a good piece of cloth.

Then a crab saw the boy. "What have you?" said the crab.

"It is cloth for my new coat," said the boy.

"I will cut the cloth," said the crab. So he cut the cloth with his feet.

(Norse Folk Fore)

译文

小男孩的外套（1）

有一个小男孩很穷，连一件外套都没有。虽然外面很冷，但他不得不在户外工作。有一天，他遇见了一只黑色的小羊羔。小羊羔说："你需要一件外套，我可以把我背上的羊毛分给你一些。"

"谢谢你。"小男孩说。

"让我来帮你把这些羊毛织起来吧，"蜘蛛说，"我可以织一张漂亮的网。"很快，蜘蛛就织出了一块很漂亮的布。

这时，一只螃蟹看到了小男孩。"你拿的是什么？"螃蟹问道。

"这是我新外套的布料。"小男孩回答说。

"我可以帮你裁布。"螃蟹说。于是，他便用两个钳子裁好了这块布。

（挪威民间传说）

Lesson 55

The Little Boy's Coat (2)

The little boy next met a bird with some yarn.

"What have you?" the bird said.

"I have cloth for my new coat," the boy said.

"Let me sew it for you. I know how to sew my nest, and I can sew your coat."

She took a long piece of yarn in her bill.

In and out, in and out, she made the yarn go.

By and by the coat was done. The little boy then put it on, and ran home.

"Father, Mother, see!" he said. "This new coat is mine. A lamb gave me the wool, and a spider, a crab, and a bird made it for me."

Then his brother and his sister came to look at it.

"We have never seen a better one!" they all said.

(Norse Folk Fore)

译文

小男孩的外套（2）

接下来，小男孩遇见了一只拿着纱线的小鸟。

"你拿的是什么？"小鸟问道。

"是做新外套的布料。"小男孩答道。

"我来帮你把布料缝起来吧。我知道如何筑巢，所以我也能做好你的外套。"

她用尖尖的嘴叼起了一根长长的纱线。

缝进，缝出，缝进，缝出，纱线在小鸟的巧嘴下不断游走。

不久，外套就做好了。小男孩穿上了外套，向家里跑去。

"爸爸，妈妈，你们快看！"他喊道，"这件新外套是我的。一只小羊羔给了我羊毛，然后蜘蛛、螃蟹和小鸟帮我把羊毛做成了衣服。"

然后，小男孩的弟弟妹妹都过来看他的新外套。

"我们还没见过比这更好的外套呢！"他们一起说道。

（挪威民间传说）

Lesson 56

"Willy boy, Willy boy,
Where are you going?
I will go with you if I may."

"I'm going to the meadow,
To see them mowing,
I'm going to help them to make the hay."

(Old English Rhymes)

译文

"小男孩,小男孩,
你要去哪里?
我可不可以随你去?"

"我要去牧场,
去看他们割草,
我要帮他们晒制干草。"

(英语传统儿歌)

Lesson 57

Rose and Amy are in their playroom.
"What would you like to play, Amy?"
"Let's play hunt the thimble."
Rose hides the thimble.
"Is it back of the clock, Rose?"
"No, Amy. Try again, you are cold."
Amy looks in the little work-box.
"Now you are getting warm, Amy."
Soon Amy finds it under the rug.

译文

罗斯和艾米正在游戏室里。
"艾米,你想玩什么?"
"我们玩找顶针的游戏吧。"
罗斯把顶针藏了起来。
"罗斯,顶针在钟后面吗?"
"不是的,艾米。再试试,你猜得有点远了。"
艾米又翻了翻小工具箱。
"现在你猜得差不多了,艾米。"
很快,艾米在毯子下找到了顶针。

Lesson 58

Rose lost her shoe one morning. She had left it in the grass.

Two little birds were looking for a house. They found the shoe.

"This is just what we wish," they said.

Date in the day Rose Went to look for the shoe. What do you think that she saw?

She saw two little heads peeping over the top of the shoe. The two little birds were in bed. They had made a nest that day.

Rose came running to tell her mother about the nest.

"Oh! Mother, may the dear little birds not keep the shoe." she said. "It is an old one. It has a hole in the side."

Her mother said, "It would be too bad to make the birds leave their house. They may keep the shoe."

译文

一天早上,罗斯丢了一只鞋。她把鞋子落在了草丛里。

两只小鸟正在找地方安家。结果,他们刚好发现了这只鞋子。

"这就是我们想找的地方呀。"他们说。

后来,罗斯去找丢失的鞋子。猜猜看,她看到了什么?

她看到,有两个小脑袋从鞋子里偷偷探了出来。两只小鸟在睡觉呢。他们看到鞋子的当天,就在鞋里筑了个巢。

罗斯赶忙跑回家,把这件事告诉了妈妈。

"哦!妈妈,别让这两只可爱的小鸟用我的那只鞋吧。"罗斯说,"这鞋子旧了,有一侧还有一个洞呢。"

罗斯的妈妈说:"逼小鸟搬家可不是好事。还是让他们用着那只鞋吧。"

Lesson 59

Here is a pretty little nest,
Soft and warm and round.
Resting in the downy bed,
Little birds are found.

"Peep! Peep! Dear, so dear!"
"Hush, my birdies, mother's near."

译文

瞧，这里有一个漂亮的小窝，
柔软、温暖的小圆窝。
这张铺满绒毛的小床，是谁的休憩之所？
呀，原来是几只小鸟的巢穴。

"唧唧！唧唧！好害怕，好害怕！"
"不怕，我的宝宝，妈妈就在你们身边。"

Lesson 60

Wishing

See this gay bed of primroses !

When these bright little flowers come, we know that it is spring.

Primroses are white or red or yellow, but most of them are yellow.

Cowslips are sometimes called primroses. Did you ever find any?

Ring-ting! I wish I were a primrose,
A bright yellow primrose blowing in the spring.

(William Allingham)

译文

愿望

看这迎春花多么鲜艳美丽！
这些鲜艳的小花绽放的时候，我们就知道春天来了。
迎春花有白色的、红色的，还有黄色的，以黄色的居多。
也有人把西洋樱草叫作迎春花。你见过吗？

啊哈！真希望变成一朵迎春花，
一朵送来春的气息的黄色小花。

（威廉·阿林厄姆）

Lesson 61

"Where do you come from, Mr. Jay?"

"From the land of Play,
From the land of Play."

"And where can that be, Mr. Jay?"

"Far away-far away."

"Where do you come from, Mrs. Dove?"

"From the land of Love,
From the land of Love."

"And how do you get there, Mrs. Dove?"

"Look above —— look above."

(L. Alma Tadema)

译文

"松鸦先生,您从哪里来?"
"从游戏的国度而来,
从游戏的国度而来。"
"那是哪里呢,松鸦先生?"
"一个很远很远的地方。"

"鸽子夫人,您从哪里来?"
"从爱的国度而来,
从爱的国度而来。"
"那你是怎么到达那里的呢,鸽子夫人?"
"抬头看看——抬头看看。"

(劳伦斯·阿尔玛·塔德玛)

思考

天上有多少颗星星?能不能告诉我你的答案?

Lesson 62

The Rooster and the Gold

A rooster was out in the yard.

"I wish that I could find some corn," he said. "Ho! ho! What is this?"

There was something on the ground. It was yellow and bright. It was hard and round. The rooster put his foot on it.

"This is mine," he said. "I shall not let the hens have it. What a queer thing it is!"

Was it corn? No, it was a bit of gold.

"I wish it were corn," the rooster said, "then I could eat it. This yellow thing is of no use."

(*Aesop*, adapted)

译文

公鸡与金子

院子里有只公鸡。

"希望我能找到些玉米,"他说道,"嘿!嘿!这是什么?"

地上有个东西。又黄又圆,硬硬的,闪闪发光。公鸡用爪子抓住它。

"好了,这是我的了。"他说,"我才不会让那群母鸡拿到它呢。这东西真奇怪呀!"

这个东西是玉米吗?不,那是一小块金子。

"这要是玉米就好了,"公鸡说,"玉米能吃呀。这个黄色的东西有什么用呢?"

(《伊索寓言》,有删改)

Lesson 63

Some little mice sat in a barn to spin.
Pussy came by, and she popped her head in.
"Shall I come in and cut your threads off?"
"Oh, no, kind sir, you will snap our heads off."

译文

几只小老鼠坐在谷仓纺纱。
一只小猫咪经过这里,把脑袋探了进去。
"我可以进去帮你们把线咬断吗?"
"哦,不,善良的先生,您会把我们的脖子咬断的。"

Lesson 64   Review

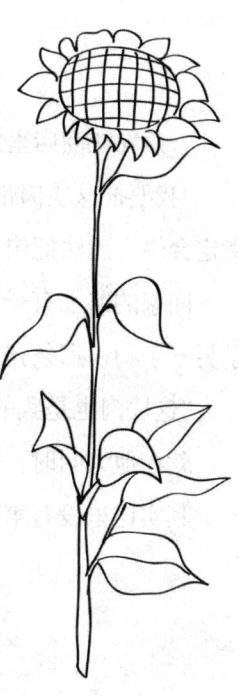

A dog found a piece of meat in a shop. He took the meat and ran away as fast as he could.

"I shall carry this home," he said. "The man in the shop may see me, and try to take it from me."

On his way home, he had to go over a small brook. Just as he was going over, he looked down into the brook. In the water he saw a dog with a piece of meat.

"I must have that meat, too," he barked. "I will take it from that dog."

As he barked, he let his own piece fall, and it was lost in the water.

There was no other dog. What had this dog seen?

(*Aesop*, adapted)

译文（复习课）

一条狗在商店里发现了一块肉。他叼起那块肉，撒腿就跑。

"我要把这块肉带回家。"他心想，"万一店里的那个家伙看到了我，肯定会想方设法把肉从我手里抢回去的。"

回家的路上有一条小河。他正准备跳过河，一低头，他在水里看到了另一条狗，那条狗也叼着一块肉。

"这块肉也是我的。"他大叫道，"得从那条狗嘴里抢过来才行。"

就在他大叫时，他嘴里叼着的那块肉掉了下去，被水冲走了。

其实这里没有第二条狗。那么，这条狗看到的又是什么呢？

（《伊索寓言》，有删改）

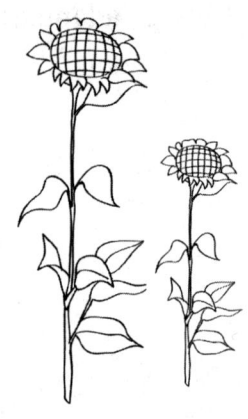

Chapter 6 | 第六章

Lesson 65

Spring had come, and the birds were with her. The brooks and the pussy-willows were awake.

The grass was out of bed. But the flowers were still sleeping.

"Come," said spring to the seed. "You must not be the last. Send up your plants. You must catch up with the grass."

Now the plants went to work. They sent little roots into the ground. They sent little stems into the air.

Up, up, the stems went. Soon they had many little leaves. Then the rain gave them water to wash their hands, and to drink.

The bright sun made their leaves green, and helped them to grow.

译文

春天到了,鸟儿来了。沉睡了一冬的小溪和柳条也醒了。

小草起床了。而花朵还在沉睡。

"来吧。"春天对种子说,"你可不能落到后面。快快把苗儿叫醒,你得赶上青草的脚步。"

于是苗儿也醒了过来。他们把小小的根伸进了土壤,把小小的茎伸到了空中。

长啊,长啊,小小的茎不停地长。很快,他们就长出了叶子。接着,雨水来了,清洗了他们的手臂,又为他们送来了甘霖。

在阳光温暖的照耀下,叶子也长得愈发青翠、愈发茁壮了。

Lesson 66

"Spring is coming!" the birds sang.

All the plants had flowers now. One had a rose, one had a peony.

Some had buttercups, some had bluebells, some had other flowers.

The little girls came to pick them. The bees came to get honey. The west wind came to play.

All the summer the flowers were working. They had to make seeds. By and by autumn came. Jack Frost was coming, too.

Kate and Tom went to garden to get seeds. They put some into a box to keep. They took some to school to plant.

The birds took some of seeds to eat. The wind put the rest away in the ground to sleep.

Little Jack Frost walked through the tress. "Oh," said the flowers, "we freeze, we freeze."

"Oh," said the grasses, "we die, we die."

Said little Jack Frost, "Good-bye, good-bye."

译文

"春天来啦！"鸟儿们唱道。

苗儿都开花了。瞧，这儿开了朵玫瑰，那儿长了株牡丹。

有毛茛，也有风信子，还有别的花儿。

小姑娘们都出来采花了。小蜜蜂们都过来采蜜了。还有那西风，也过来玩耍了。

整个夏天，花朵们都在绽放。他们要结出种子来。慢慢地，秋天到了。之后，寒冬也来了。

凯特和汤姆来花园收集种子。采回来的种子，一部分被放进了盒子里，用来收藏。还有一部分被他们带到了学校，用来种植。

小鸟儿也吃掉了一些种子。剩下的，被风儿吹进了土里，静静安睡。

寒冬从树丛边悄悄走过。"哦！"花儿们说，"我们要冻僵了，我们要冻僵了。"

"哦，"草儿们说，"我们要冻死了，我们要冻死了。"

寒冬则对他们说："再见吧，朋友们，再见。"

Lesson 67

Little Brown Brother

Little brown brother, oh! Little brown brother,
  Are you awake in the dark?
  Here in the ground we lie close to each other,
  Do hear the song of the lark.

Little brown brother, oh! Little brown brother,
  What kind of flower will you be?
  I am a peony —— all red, like my mother;
    Do be a peony like me.

  Are you a sunflower? How I shall miss you——
  When you grow up so yellow and high!
  But I shall send all the bees up to kiss you.
  Little brown brother, good-bye.

(E. Nesbit)

译文

棕色的朋友

嘿,我棕色的朋友,我棕色的朋友,
你是否在黑夜醒来?
瞧,我们在泥土里,紧紧抱成一团,
一起倾听百灵鸟的歌唱。

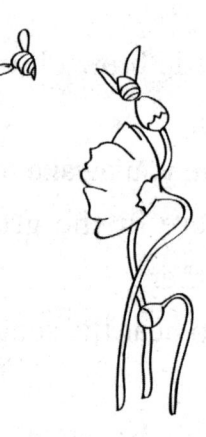

嘿,我棕色的朋友,我棕色的朋友,
你是什么花呢?
我是牡丹花——火红的牡丹花,就像我的妈妈,
长得跟我一样的牡丹花。

你是向日葵吗?我该有多么想念你——
等你长高长大,开出黄色的花。
不过等到那个时候,我会让所有的蜜蜂都来亲吻你。
再会了我棕色的朋友,再会吧。

(伊迪丝·内斯比特)

Lesson 68

See, the sun is shining through the rain! Perhaps we shall have a rainbow.

Oh, there is a rainbow now! What pretty colors it has! Red and blue and yellow.

It is said that there is a pot of gold at the end of the rainbow. Do you think you ever could find it?

How sweet the color is after the rain!

译文

看,阳光在雨滴间闪耀呢!或许我们能看到彩虹了。

哦,彩虹出现了!瞧它的色彩是多么的美丽!红色、蓝色,还有黄色。

据说,在彩虹的尽头有一桶金子。你觉得你能找到吗?

哦,雨后的色彩是多么迷人啊!

Lesson 69

The Clovers

The clovers have no time to play:
They feed the cows and make the hay,
And trim the lawns and help the bees,
Until the sun sinks through the trees.
And then they drop their little heads,
And go to sleep in clover beds.
Then when the day dawns clear and blue,
They wake and wash their lands in dew.
And as the sun climbs up the sky,
They mold them up and let them dry,
And then to work the livelong day,
For clovers have no time to play.

译文

三叶草

三叶草，忙不停：
喂奶牛，晒干草，
修草坪，帮蜜蜂，
太阳下山才罢休。
小脑袋，轻轻垂，
小小床儿好入睡。
夜走了，天亮了，
三叶草儿忙梳洗。
太阳公公已出山，
快把露水晒晒干，
好把活儿继续干，
因为三叶草们忙不完。

Lesson 70

Fanny's cousin had a birthday party. But Fanny was sick, and could not go.

"Let us have a snow party," her mother said. Fanny clapped her hands.

Her mother put a black cloth in an open window. Down came the flakes.

Fanny's mother then gave her the cloth. "Count the flakes, Fanny," she said. "They have come to your party."

Stars came, and Flowers, and Roses, and White Flakes, and many others.

译文

范尼的表姐举办了一个生日派对。但范尼生病了,没去成。

"我们办一个雪花派对吧。"范尼的妈妈说。听到这话范尼开心地拍起了手。

于是妈妈打开了窗户,挂了一块黑色的布。很快,就有小雪花落在了布上。

范尼的妈妈把布给了范尼,"范尼,数数看有多少雪花。"妈妈说,"他们都是来参加你的派对的。"

于是,星星来了,花儿来了,玫瑰来了,白色的小雪花来了,还有好多其他客人,也都来了。

思考

说说看你看到了哪些形状的雪花?

Lesson 71

This doe and her little fawn have come to the edge of the field to drink.

Doe is the name we give to a mother deer. We call a little deer a fawn.

What short tails and what big ears deer have, and what a pretty, soft color their coats are!

If only we could touch the little fawn! But we must stand very still. If we move, he will run away.

译文

母鹿和她的宝宝来田野边找水喝。

鹿妈妈叫作雌鹿,而那些小鹿叫作幼鹿。

瞧,鹿的尾巴多短,耳朵多大呀!它们的皮毛又漂亮又柔软!

要是我们能摸摸那只幼鹿该多好啊!不过我们一定要安安静静地站着。否则,我们一动,鹿就会跑掉啦。

Lesson 72

A Sea Song

Hail! Ho! Sail! Ho!
Ahoy! Ahoy! Ahoy!
Who calls to me,
So far at sea?
Only a little boy!
Sail! Ho! Hail! Ho!
The sailor sails the sea.
I wish he would capture
A little sea-horse,
And send him home to me.

(James Whitcomb Riley)

 译文

海洋之歌

万岁！嘿！起航啦！嘿！

喂！喂！喂！
听，那遥远的海上，
是谁在叫我？
原来是一个小男孩！
万岁！嘿！起航啦！嘿！
水手出海了。
真希望他能抓一只
小小的海马，
把它从海里带回给我。

（詹姆斯·惠特科姆·莱里）

朗读

Water now is turned to stone,
Stone that I can walk upon.

(Robert Louis Stevenson)

河水结冰了，
我可以在冰上行走了。

（罗伯特·路易斯·斯蒂文森）

Lesson 73

This boy was sent to a field to take care of a flock of sheep. Not far away some farmers were at work on a farm.

"If a wolf comes, call to us," a farmer said, "we will help you."

No wolf came that day. The next day the boy said, "I shall have some sport." So he called, "Wolf, wolf!"

The men left their work, and ran to catch the wolf. "Oh, I was only in fun," the boy said. "I have not seen a wolf."

The same day the boy called again, "Wolf, wolf!"

The men again ran quickly. The boy laughed at the men. "I was only in fun," he said again.

The next day a wolf did come. Then the boy called as loud as he could.

"Do not fear," said one man. "He is in fun." So the men did not go to him. And the bad wolf took one of the lambs.

(Aesop, adapted)

译文

  有个小男孩在田边放羊。在不远处,有一些农民正在田间干活。

  "如果有狼过来,记得叫我们,"有一个农民说,"我们会过来帮你。"

  这一整天都没有狼过来。第二天,小男孩无聊了,他想:"我要找点乐子。"于是,他大声喊道:"狼来了!狼来了!"

  田间的农民们赶忙放下手中的活,跑来帮小男孩抓狼。"哦,我只是开了个玩笑,"小男孩说,"我可没看到什么狼。"

  这一天晚些时候,小男孩又大声叫道:"狼来了!狼来了!"

  农民们又急匆匆地赶了过来。小男孩却哈哈大笑了起来:"我只是开个玩笑而已。"

  第二天,真的有一只狼来了。小男孩使出了全身力气大声喊道:"狼来了!狼来了!"

  "别担心。"一个农民说,"他只是在开玩笑。"于是,人们没有去帮小男孩。那只狼就把小男孩的一只羊叼走了。

(《伊索寓言》,有删改)

Lesson 74

The Mice and the Cat

There was an old cat who kill all the mice she could catch.

The little mice feared that she would kill every one of them. They feared that there would not be one mouse left.

So one day the mice met in a barn. They met to talk about how they could keep out of the old cat's way.

"Do as I say," said one wise old mouse with a gray beard. "Do as I say. Let us hang a bell to the cat's neck. When we hear it ring, we shall know the cat is coming. Then we will run."

"Good! Good!" said all the rest of the mice. And they ran to get the hell.

"Now who will hang it to the cat's neck?" said wise old Gray Beard.

"Not I! Not I!" said all the mice at one time.

(*Aesop*, adapted)

译文

猫和老鼠

有一只老猫,老鼠只要落入她的掌中,就难逃一死。

小老鼠们都怕死在她手上。他们心惊胆战,觉得再这样下去,他们都会被吃掉的。

于是有一天,老鼠们聚在了谷仓,一起商量怎么躲开那只老猫。

"照我说啊,"一只白胡须的聪明老鼠说道,"照我说啊,我们应该往猫的脖子上挂一个铃铛。这样,一听到铃铛的声音,我们就知道猫来了。我们就逃之夭夭吧。"

"好主意!好主意!"其他的老鼠都欢呼道。于是他们就跑去找铃铛了。

"那么,谁去把铃铛挂到猫的脖子上呢?"刚刚那只白胡须的聪明老鼠问道。

"别找我!我不行!"所有老鼠都异口同声地说道。

(《伊索寓言》,有删改)

Lesson 75 Review

Some ants had their home in an ant-hill. The ant-hill was close to a brook.

One morning a little ant fell into the brook. No one could hear her call. Her sisters were all at work in the fields.

"I shall never get out," the ant said.

Just then a dove saw her. He was on a tree above the brook. "I will help you," he said. So he picked off a leaf, and let it drop into the brook.

The ant climbed up on the leaf. She was soon out of the water.

Not long after this a man with a gun saw the dove. "I must get that dove," he said.

But the ant had seen the man. She ran to him, and bit him on the hand.

This made him move his gun. Then the dove saw him, and flew away.

(Aesop, adapted)

译文（复习课）

蚂蚁山的旁边有一条小河。山上住了一群蚂蚁。

一天早上，一只小蚂蚁不小心摔到了河里。没人听到她的呼救声。她的姐妹们那时正在地里忙着干活呢。

"我肯定出不去了。"小蚂蚁想。

就在这时，一只鸽子看到了她。鸽子就住在河上的一棵树上。"我会帮你的。"鸽子说。于是，他摘下了一片叶子，丢进河里。

小蚂蚁爬上那片叶子，很快就从水里逃了出来。

没多久，一个拿着枪的人看到了鸽子。"我得打下那只鸽子。"他心想。

但是小蚂蚁看到了这个人。她立即冲向那个人，在他手上狠狠地咬了一口。

于是，枪打偏了。这时，鸽子看见了猎人，就飞走了。

（《伊索寓言》，有删改）

Chapter 7 | 第七章

Lesson 76

The Home of a Rabbit

Let me tell you about this rabbit home.

The rabbit first made a hole on the ground. This was her house. She next put a roof of grass on it. Then she made a little bed for the baby rabbits.

The bed was dry and warm. It was made of soft fur. The mother rabbit took the fur from her own coat.

One I went with a friend to visit the rabbits. We had to lift up the little cover of grass.

Five tiny rabbits were at home.

译文

兔子的家

我们来说说兔子的家吧。

开始,兔子在地上挖了一个洞。这是她的房子。接着,她又在洞里铺了一层草。后来她又给小兔子们做了张小床。

小床干燥温暖,是用柔软的毛做成的。这些毛是兔子妈妈从自己的身上拔下来的。

有一次,我和朋友去看望兔子一家。我们得翻开洞口上的草才能看见他们。

有五只小兔子躺在家里。

Lesson 77

Little Bunny Pink-Eye,
Out for a hop,
Let me catch you, Bunny sweet,
Stop, stop, stop!

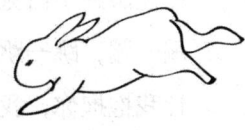

    All about the clover-bed,
    Eating fast and slow,
    Stop, my little Bunny sweet,
    let the clovers grow.

    Some are pink like Bunny's eyes,
Full of honey new;
Some are white like Bunny's ears,
Full of morning dew.
Let them grove, my Bunny sweet,
Till some other day,
Then come back with hop and jump,
And eat them all away.

                    (L. E. Orth , adapted)

译文

粉色眼睛小白兔,
蹦一蹦,跳一跳,小兔小兔出来了。
让我抱抱你,我亲爱的小白兔。
哦,不、不、不!
你看这么多的小苜蓿,
你可要慢点儿吃,
慢一点,我的小白兔,
小苜蓿们也要长大成熟。

瞧这里,粉粉的,就像你的大眼睛,
甜甜的蜜儿里面藏;
看那里,白白的,就像你的长耳朵,
都是清晨的朝露。
让他们好好长大吧,我亲爱的小白兔,
待他们都成熟,
你再来蹦,再来跳,
再把它们都吃进肚。

(L. E. 奥斯,有删改)

Lesson 78

Girls and boys, come out to play.

The moon doth shine as bright as day.

Come with a whoop, come with a call.

Come with a good-will or not at all.

(*Mother Goose*, adapted)

译文

男孩女孩出来玩。

月光亮得如白天。

伴一声呼哨，伴一声喊叫。

伴一个美好愿望，否则就不要。

（《鹅妈妈》，有删改）

Lesson 79

The Little Fir Tree

Long ago a little fir tree lived in the woods. Near it were many large trees.

"Why am I not so big as the other trees?" the little fir would ask. "I wish to be big."

After a while men came and cut down most of the big trees, and took them away.

"Where have they gone?" said the fir.

"We saw them far away on a ship," the birds said.

"I wish that I could be on a ship," said the little tree.

"Please do not go away," said the birds and sunbeams. "We should miss you very much. We need you here."

At last, winter came. Snow and ice were on the ground. The air was cold.

Then two boys came into the woods and cut down the little fir tree.

They put it on their sled, and then they pulled the sled over the snow.

The tree was soon in a large room. Pretty things were hung all over it.

The next morning everyone was very happy. The little fir had something to give everyone.

The children had candy and toys. There were dolls and balls, sleds and skates, and all kinds of things. Baby had horse. Father and Mother had books.

Now the little fir was happy.

When its work was done, it was put safely away in a dark room. A mouse lived in this room. And every day the little tree told the mouse a little story.

(*Hans Christian Adersen*, adapted)

译文

一棵小枞树

很久以前，森林里有一棵小枞树。它的周围长了许多大树。

"为什么我不像其他树一样高大呢？"小枞树疑惑地问道，"我想长成一棵大树。"

过了一会儿，森林里来了一群人，他们砍倒了大部分大树，然后把他们带走了。

"他们去哪儿了？"小枞树问道。

"我们看见他们乘船离开了。"鸟儿们回答说。

"我希望我能成为一艘船。"小枞树轻声说。

"请你不要离开，"鸟儿和阳光一同说道，"我们都会非常想念你。我们需要你呀。"

终于，冬天来了。地上结了冰，积满了雪。天气很冷。

这一天，森林里来了两个小男孩，他们砍倒了小枞树。

他们把小树放在了雪橇上，拉着雪橇离开了。

不久，小树就来到了一间宽敞的屋子。它身上挂满了漂亮的装饰。

第二天早上，每个人都很开心。因为小枞树把礼物送给了每一个人。

孩子们都拿到了糖果和玩具，还有玩具娃娃、球、雪橇、冰鞋和其他东西。小宝宝得到了木马，爸爸妈妈则收到了书。

小枞树现在觉得很快乐。

等小枞树完成了使命,它就被小心翼翼地收进了一间小黑屋里。小黑屋里住着一只老鼠。从此,小枞树每天都会给小老鼠讲一个小故事。

(《安徒生童话》,有删改)

Lesson 80

"Chip, Chip!"

One morning I went to pick strawberries. Before long my tin cup was full.

Then I set the cup down and went to the brook for a drink.

A little brown squirrel saw my cup. He ran quickly to find out what was in it. Soon he was on the cup.

He took one berry. Then he took two. "Chip, chip, chip!" he said. "They are good. It will be better to fill my pockets."

A squirrel's pockets are in his cheeks.

Two, four, six, seven, eight, of my strawberries were quickly gone. His cheeks looked very fat. My berries were in his pockets.

All this time he kept eating. Then he ran away to tell his friends about his dinner.

(John Burroughs)

译文

"吱吱，吱吱！"

一天早晨，我去采草莓。不一会儿，我的锡杯就满了。

于是，我把杯子放在了地上，去小溪边喝水。

一只灰色的小松鼠看到了我的杯子。他连忙跑了过来，好像要看看杯子里有什么东西。不一会儿，他就站在了杯口上。

他拿起了一颗草莓。然后他又拿起了第二颗。"吱吱，吱吱，吱吱！"他说，"草莓真好吃。要是能把这些草莓都装到我的小口袋里去就好了！"

小松鼠的小口袋，就在他的两颊里。

两个，四个，六个，七个，八个，我的草莓不一会儿就没了。他的两颊也鼓了起来。我的草莓全到他的两颊里去啦。

他一直吃呀吃呀。之后，他就跑去和朋友讲这顿饱餐的故事了。

（约翰·巴勒斯）

Lesson 81

Clytie was a fairy. Her home was in the deep sea.

She had a pretty wagon. It was made of a pink shell. She had a fish to draw her wagon.

One day Clytie went to drive. Soon she came to the top of the water.

Then Clytie saw the sky and the sun. She got out on the land. She looked at the sun all day. But at last it went out of her sight in the west.

The next day she came again, and the next days and the next. Then what do you think?

She found that she could not move. Her feet were fast in the ground.

Her green dress was turned into a green stem. Her yellow hair was turned into a flower.

Clytie was glad. Now she could stay on the earth. So all day she keeps her face to the sun.

(Greek Myth)

译文

　　克吕提厄是一位仙女。她住在深海里。

　　她有一辆很漂亮的马车。马车是用粉色的贝壳做成的。一条鱼给她驾车。

　　有一天,克吕提厄乘车出游。很快,她就到达了水面。

　　于是,克吕提厄看到了美丽的天空和太阳,就踏上了岸。一整天,她都紧紧地盯着太阳。但最后,太阳还是在西方的天空中消失了。

　　第二天,她又来了,第三天,第四天,以后的每一天她都会来这里。猜猜最后发生了什么事情?

　　她突然发现自己动不了了。她的双脚深深地陷入了土壤之中。

　　她的绿裙子变成了绿色的茎,而她那金黄的头发变成了花盘。

　　克吕提厄很高兴。现在,她可以永远待在陆地上了。于是,她永远面向太阳,每日追随。

(《希腊神话》)

Lesson 82

Brer Rabbit

Brer Rabbit went to see Mr. Bear. "I think that I shall stay for supper?" said Brer Rabbit. "That will please Mr. Bear."

Mr. Bear Was not at home. Then Brer Rabbit was up to old tricks.

"I don't want to wait for Mr. Bear," he said. "He may not come until tonight. But I must have lunch now."

So Brer Rabbit went into the storeroom. Mr. Bear's storeroom was full.

"I smell honey," said Brer Rabbit. He tried to deep into the boxes. A jug of honey fell down on him.

"What shall I do?" said Brer Rabbit. "Let me think. I will go down to those trees. I will roll on those leaves."

So Brer Rabbit went to the trees.

He lay down under a bush. He tried to rub the honey off on the ground.

He tried to wipe it off on the grass.

He tried in every way to get rid of it. But he only got leaves and sticks all over him.

How funny did he look! The cow saw him and ran. The wolf saw him and ran. The bear saw him and ran.

(Joel Chandler Harris)

译文

贝尔兔

贝尔兔去看熊先生。"我是不是得在熊先生家吃晚餐呀?"贝尔兔想,"在他家吃晚餐的话,熊先生肯定会很开心。"

然而熊先生并不在家。于是贝尔兔玩起了老把戏。

"我不想等熊先生,"他说,"他可能晚上才能回来。但我现在就得吃午饭了。"

于是,贝尔兔走进熊先生的储藏室。储藏室里满满的都是食物。

"我闻到了蜂蜜的味道,"贝尔兔说。他便开始翻储藏室里的盒子。结果他碰倒了一罐蜂蜜,洒得一身都是。

"我该怎么办?"贝尔兔说,"让我想想。我得去那边的灌木丛。在叶子上滚几圈,就能把蜂蜜擦干净了。"

于是,贝尔兔跑到树丛里。

他躺倒在灌木丛下。他努力想把蜂蜜擦到地上。他又试着用草把身上的蜂蜜擦干净。

为了把蜂蜜弄掉,他试了各种各样的方法。但最后,他只是沾了一身的叶子和树枝而已。

瞧,他看着多滑稽啊!奶牛看到他吓跑了。狼看到他吓跑了。连熊看到他也吓跑了。

(乔尔·钱乐德·哈里斯)

Lesson 83

The Three Wishes

Nell came in from the garden. She had a basket on her arm.

"Oh, Mamma! Let us play that you are a poor lady. I am a fairy, and I will give you three wishes.

"You must not wish for any big thing. You must wish for a rose, or a cherry or something that I can carry in my basket."

"I hardly know what to wish," said Mamma. "Let me see. I wish for a rose."

"How did you guess?" said Nell. "Here is a fresh rose."

"What a sweet rose!" said Mamma. "Thank you."

"Now wish again, Mamma."

"My second wish is for two cherries," said Mamma.

"Oh, how did you guess right?" said Nell. And she held out two cherries.

"Thank you," said Mamma. "Now I have a third wish."

"Yes," said Nell, "but I had only the rose and the cherries. I am sorry I do not know how to play one more wish."

"I do. It is very easy. I wish for a kiss." That wish came true, too. "It was the best of all," said Mamma.

(Mary M. Dodge, adapted)

译文

三个愿望

内尔从花园回来了。她的胳膊上挽着一个篮子。

"哦,妈妈!我们玩一个游戏吧,假装你是个可怜的老婆婆,我是个仙女,我能满足你的三个愿望。"

"你不能许愿要太大件的东西。你可以许愿得到玫瑰、樱桃或其他能装进我的篮子里的东西。"

"我实在不知道要许什么愿啊。"妈妈说,"让我想想。有了,我希望能有一朵玫瑰。"

"你怎么猜到的?"内尔说,"给你,刚采来的玫瑰。"

"多美的玫瑰啊!"妈妈说,"谢谢你。"

"现在再许一个愿望吧,妈妈。"

"我的第二个愿望是希望能有两颗樱桃。"妈妈说。

"哦,天啊!你怎么又猜对了?"内尔说。她拿出两颗樱桃。

"谢谢你。"妈妈说,"现在我要说第三个愿望了。"

"好的,"内尔说,"不过我只有玫瑰和樱桃。很抱歉,但我真的不知道如何实现你的其他愿望。"

"我知道。这个愿望很简单。我想要一个亲吻。"于是妈妈的这个愿望也实现了。"这是三个愿望里最好的一个。"妈妈说。

(玛丽·梅普斯·道奇,有删改)

Lesson 84

How do you like to go up in a swing,
Up in the air so blue?
Oh, I do think it the pleasantest thing
Ever a child can do!

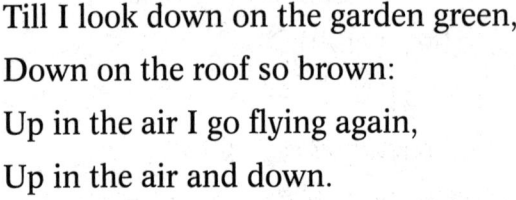

Up in the air and over the wall,
Till I can see so wide:
Rivers and trees and cattle, and all
Over the countryside.

Till I look down on the garden green,
Down on the roof so brown:
Up in the air I go flying again,
Up in the air and down.

(Robert Louis Stevenson)

译文

你喜欢荡着秋千,
飞向蓝色的晴空吗?
哦,我觉得这是小孩子能玩的
最好的游戏!

越过高墙,荡向天空,
直至我能望见这广阔的天地:
看见那清流、绿树、牛群,
还有整片乡村。

直到我能俯瞰那青翠的花园,
那褐色的屋檐。
然后我会再次飞回那片天,
穿梭于这天地与人间。

(罗伯特·路易斯·斯蒂文森)

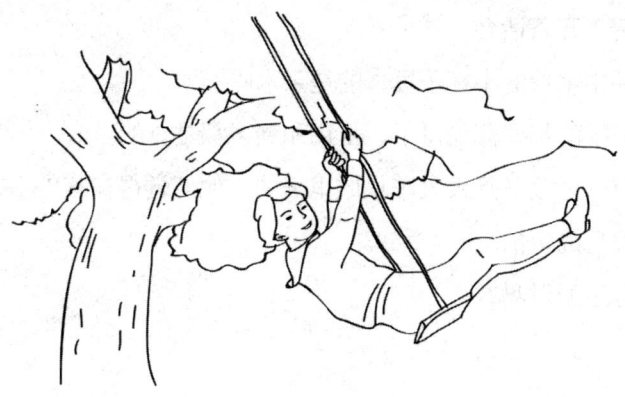

Lesson 85

These children are having a tea party out under the trees.

Do you think that they have real tea in those little cups?

They have real crackers and cakes and candy.

Some of the children have come from the city. They came on the train. They think that it is the best fun in the world to have a party out of doors.

Did you ever go to an out of doors party?

译文

孩子们正在树下开茶话会。

你觉得他们手中拿着的小杯子里真的是茶水吗?

不过他们面前摆的那些薄脆饼干、蛋糕和糖果都是真的。

他们当中,有一些孩子是乘火车从城里来的。他们觉得在室外举办派对是世界上最好玩的事情。

你在室外举办过派对吗?

Lesson 86

Nuts in a Jar

James always liked to have the best things for himself.

He took the finest apple and the largest piece of candy, and he wanted to stay longest on the swing.

One day his mother had a jar with nuts in it. "Each child may put his hand into the jar just once," she said. "James, you may try first."

James was glad to be first. "I shall take a big, big handful," he said to himself.

He put in his hand, and took as many nuts as he could

grasp. Then he tried to draw his hand out. It would not come. The neck of the jar was too small.

He tried again, but his hand was fast. He began to cry, for he did not like to give up the nuts.

The other children laughed, but his mother was sorry that he was so greedy. "Drop some of the nuts," she said, "then you can take out the pest."

James did as his mother told him. But he had to drop so many nuts, that he had only his share.

(Aesop, adapted)

✎ 译文

罐子里的坚果

詹姆斯总喜欢把最好的东西给自己享用。

他会拿走最好吃的苹果、最大块的糖,每次荡秋千时,他也希望自己是荡得最久的那个。

有一天,妈妈拿来了一个罐子,罐子里装满了坚果。"每个小孩只能拿一次坚果,"妈妈说,"詹姆斯,你第一个来吧。"

能第一个拿坚果,这让詹姆斯很高兴。"我要拿满满的、满满的一大把坚果。"他自言自语道。

他把手伸进罐子里,然后把手张到最大,想拿到最多的坚果。等他想把手抽出来的时候,却发现罐子的颈部太小了,手根本抽不出来。

他又试了一下,却发现手被卡得紧紧的。可是詹姆斯实在不想放开手中的坚果,于是他哭了起来。

其他的孩子看着詹姆斯的样子都哈哈大笑起来,但妈妈却因詹姆斯的贪婪感到难过。"把手里的坚果丢掉一些,"妈妈说,"这样你才能把手拿出来。"

詹姆斯按妈妈说的做了。但他不得不把大部分坚果放下,手里只剩下了一小份。

(《伊索寓言》,有删改)

Lesson 87

O dandelion, yellow as gold.
What do you do all day?
I just wait here in the long green grass,
Till the children come to play.

O dandelion, yellow as gold.
What do you do all night?
I wait and wait while the cool dew falls,
And my hair grows long and white.

(Mrs. E.P. Erskine)

译文

蒲公英，黄如金。
白天的你，忙什么？
我在青草间等呀等，
等着小朋友们来玩耍。

蒲公英，黄如金。
黑夜的你，做什么？
我还在等，等着朝露来降临，
等到我的发丝长长又染霜。

（E. P. 厄斯金夫人）

Lesson 88

A blue jay once found some bright peacock's feathers in a barnyard. He stuck them in his tail. He felt very proud.

"How fine I look!" he said. "I will not live with the blue jays anymore. I will live with the peacocks."

But the peacocks only laughed at the little foolish bird. So he went back to the jays, but they would not let him come among them.

译文

一只蓝松鸦在仓院里发现了些孔雀羽毛，亮亮的，颜色很漂亮。于是，他便把这些羽毛插到了尾巴上。看着自己的杰作，小蓝松鸦可骄傲了。

"瞧，我看起来多美啊！"他说，"我再也不是蓝松鸦了。以后我就能当上一只孔雀啦。"

但是，孔雀们嘲笑这只愚蠢的鸟。于是，他只能回到松鸦群里，但松鸦们也不再接纳他了。

Lesson 89

A Little Bird

There was once a little bird,
So full of song,
That she sang in the rose-bush,
The whole night long.

And "Oh!" said the redbird to the jay,
"Don't you wish you could sit,
And sing that way?"

"Mercy, no!" said the jay,
"For he sings too late;
I sing well enough to please my mate."

Then "Oh!" said the redbird to the crow,
"Don't you wish you could sit,
And sing just so?"

"Do hush," said the crow,
"Or I'll begin to weep,

Be-caw-caw-cause he is
Losing his sleep."

(Joel Chandler Harris)

译文

一只小鸟

曾有一只小小鸟,
全神贯注把歌唱,
她在玫瑰丛中唱,
整夜唱不停。

红雀看到小松鸡,
"小松鸡,小松鸡,要不要坐过去,
像他一样把歌唱?"

"谢谢,谢谢,不用了!"松鸡说,
"因为已太晚;
我美妙的歌声也只为取悦我的另一半。"

红雀又看见了大乌鸦,
"大乌鸦,大乌鸦,要不要去那里,

像他一样歌唱?"

"别出声,"乌鸦说,
"不然我的眼泪又要流,
因——因——因为啊,
他一直一直睡不好。"

(乔尔·钱德勒·哈里斯)

Lesson 90

Mufflu(1)

Lolo was a little lame boy ten years old. His home was in a large city far over the sea.

Lolo's father was dead, and his mother was very poor. Lolo's big brother Tasso had to work hard to take care of his mother, and his little brothers and sisters.

Mufflu was Lolo's pet dog. The two were close friends. Mufflu was small, and had long white hair like soft wool.

One morning Lolo and his dog were playing near their home. A gentleman saw them.

"You have a fine dog there, my little man," he said to Lolo. "Does he know any tricks?"

"Oh, yes!" said Lolo. "Mufflu can walk on two legs, play that he is dead, dance, beg, open a door, and play soldier. Would you like to see him in something?"

"Yes, very much," said the gentleman.

So Lolo put Mufflu through his tricks. The little dog did well, and the gentleman was much pleased.

"Would you bring your dog to my house, and let my little sick boy see him?" the gentleman asked.

Lolo said that he would. So the man gave him some money, and told him how to find the house.

Lolo went home as fast as he could with his crutch. "See, Mother! A gentleman gave me this money because Mufflu did his tricks," he cried. "Now you can buy some shoes and all the things that you want."

In the afternoon Lolo and Mufflu went to the gentleman's house. Here Mufflu did all his tricks again for Victor, the sick boy.

It was great sort for Victor to see the little dog. He laughed and clapped his hands for joy, and gave both Lolo and Mufflu cakes and candy. His father gave Lolo some more money.

Victor did not want Lolo to take Mufflu away. "I want the dog! I will have the dog!" he kept saying. But Lolo could not part with Mufflu.

(Louise De La Ramee, adapted)

译文

穆夫鲁（1）

洛洛是个跛脚的十岁小男孩。他家住在一座内陆的大城市。

洛洛的爸爸去世了，他的妈妈非常穷。洛洛还有一个哥哥叫塔索，为了照顾妈妈和弟弟妹妹们，塔索非常努力地工作。

穆夫鲁是洛洛的宠物狗。他们俩是最好的朋友。穆夫鲁个子小小的，毛又白又长，软软的，像羊毛一样。

一天早晨，洛洛和小狗在家附近玩耍。一位先生看到了他们。

"小伙子，你有一条很棒的狗，"那个人对洛洛说，"他会什么绝活吗？"

"哦，当然！"洛洛答道，"穆夫鲁会直立行走，会装死，会跳舞，会讨食，会开门，还会玩打仗游戏呢。你想不想见识一下？"

"当然了，非常想。"这位先生说。

于是，洛洛让穆夫鲁表演了几个绝活。小狗漂亮地完成了，而那位先生看得也很开心。

"你可以带你的狗去我家，让我生病的儿子看看他吗？"这位先生问道。

洛洛同意了。于是，先生给了洛洛一些钱，还告诉了洛洛他家怎么走。

洛洛拿到了钱，拄着拐杖尽快走着，他想快点回家。"妈妈，看啊！一个先生给了我这些钱，因为穆夫鲁表演了几个绝活给他看。"他大喊道。

"现在你可以买几双鞋了，还能买其他东西呢。"

那天下午，洛洛和穆夫鲁一起去那位先生家。来到这儿，穆夫鲁给维克多——那位生了病的小男孩叫维克多——又表演了一次绝活。

维克多看到小狗可开心了。他开心得边笑边拍手，还给了洛洛和穆夫鲁好些蛋糕和糖果。他爸爸又给了洛洛一些钱。

维克多不想让洛洛带走穆夫鲁。"我想要这条狗！我要这条狗！"他不停地大叫道。但洛洛和穆夫鲁根本分不开。

（路易斯·德拉·拉梅，有删改）

Lesson 91

Mufflu(2)

When Lolo got home, he found everyone crying. Word had just come that Tasso must go away and be a soldier. His mother and the children would not have any one to take care of them.

"If we only had some money," his mother said, "then we could get a man to go in Tasso's place."

Lolo gave his money to his mother. But it was not enough to help her. Then he and Mufflu went off to bed, and Lolo cried himself to sleep.

The next morning the gentleman came to buy the little dog for Victor. Lolo was not at home, and his mother did not know what to do.

At last she sold Mufflu. The man gave her a great deal of money for the dog.

Now Lolo's mother was quite happy again, for she could pay a man to be a soldier in Tasso's place.

In the evening Lolo came home. "Mufflu!" he called. "Where is Mufflu?" But no little dog ran to meet him.

"Mufflu has been sold," the children said.

Poor Lolo! He turned white and fell over on the floor. His mother had to take him up and put him in bed.

He was so sick that he did not know his mother or any one at all. But he cried for Mufflu all the time.

Tasso and his mother were very sad. They sent for the doctor for Lolo.

"I fear that Lolo can not get well," the doctor said. "You must get his dog for him."

But they could not get the dog, for the gentleman had gone away with Victor and Mufflu.

The doctor came again.

This time he said, "Lolo will die."

Just then there was a patter on the stairs. In a moment a ball of mud and dust flew in, and jumped on the bed.

It was Mufflu. He had run away, and come back many, many miles to his old home.

The next day Lolo was much better.

In a few days the gentleman came to the city again. Then Tasso took the money, and went to see him.

"Mufflu has come back to us," Tasso said, "and we should like to keep him for Lolo. My little brother has been very sick. I wish to give back your money, and I will go and be a soldier."

The gentleman and Victor were sorry for Lolo.

"Keep the money, Tasso," the man said, "and train a

little dog like Mufflu for Victor."

What joy there was at home when Tasso told the good news! Lolo could keep Mufflu, and Tasso could stay and take care of them all.

After a while Lolo could walk again with his crutch. Then he and Mufflu had merry times.

Every day, they went to play with Victor and the puppy that Tasso was training for Victor.

(Louise De La Ramee, adapted)

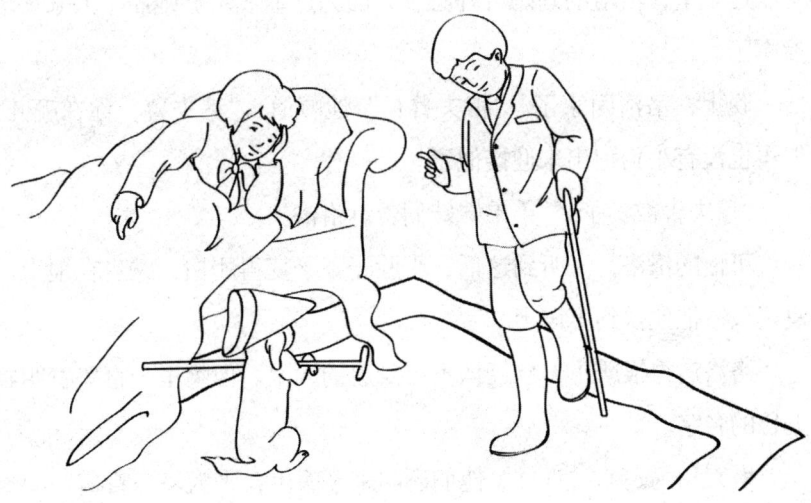

译文

穆夫鲁（2）

洛洛回到家后，发现家里人都在哭。原来，有人说，塔索必须去参军。这样一来，再也没有人照顾妈妈和家里的孩子了。

"要是我们有点钱就好了，"他妈妈说，"这样我们就可以找个人替塔索参军了。"

洛洛把身上的钱全部给了妈妈。但这笔钱远远不够。之后他和穆夫鲁准备上床睡觉了，可怜的小洛洛哭着睡着了。

第二天一大早，那位先生来了，他要买下这条小狗送给儿子。当时，洛洛不在家，他妈妈也不知道该如何是好。

最后，妈妈还是卖掉了穆夫鲁。那位先生给了她一大笔钱。

这下子，洛洛的妈妈可开心了，因为这笔钱足够她雇个人来替塔索参军了。

晚上，洛洛回家了。"穆夫鲁！"他喊道，"穆夫鲁，你在哪儿？"但再也没有小狗跑出来迎接他了。

"穆夫鲁被卖了。"弟弟妹妹们告诉洛洛。

可怜的洛洛，一听到这话，小脸一下子变得刷白，跌坐在地上。他妈妈只得把他扶到了床上。

洛洛病得很严重，已经认不出身边的人了。但嘴里一直哭着叫着穆夫鲁的名字。

塔索和妈妈非常难过。他们还叫来了医生，来为洛洛看病。

"我恐怕，洛洛好不了了。"医生说，"你得去把他的小狗找回来才行。"

但他们根本找不到小狗,因为那位先生早就带着维克多和穆夫鲁离开了这里。

医生又来了。

这次他说:"洛洛快死了。"

就在这时,楼梯上传来了脚步声。不一会儿,一个小泥球冲了进来,然后跳到了床上。

是穆夫鲁!他从新主人那里逃跑了,走了很长很长的路,才找到了原来的家。

第二天,洛洛就好了很多。

几天后,那位先生又来到了这座城市。塔索带着那笔钱,去见他。

"穆夫鲁回到我们身边了,"塔索说,"为了洛洛,我们得留下它。我弟弟因为穆夫鲁病得很重。所以我想把钱还给您,我会去参军的。"

这位先生和维克多听了洛洛的事情,都觉得很难过。

"这钱你拿着吧,塔索,"先生说,"然后帮维克多也训练一条像穆夫鲁那样的狗。"

塔索回到家告诉了大家这个好消息,一家人别提多开心了!洛洛可以留下穆夫鲁,而塔索也可以继续在家里照顾他们了。

没多久,洛洛就又可以拄着拐杖走路了。他跟穆夫鲁一起快乐地生活着。

每天,他们都会和维克多一起玩,对了,还有那条塔索正在训练的小狗,也和他们在一起。

(路易斯·德拉·拉梅,有删改)

Lesson 92

Father, we thank Thee for the night,
And for the pleasant morning light,
For rest and food and loving care,
And all that makes the world so fair.
Help us to do the things we should,
To be to others kind and good.
In all we do, in work or play,
To grow more loving every day.

(Rebecca Weston)

译文

慈爱的天父,感谢您赐予我们这良夜,
还有那晨光的喜悦。
感谢您赐予我们休息、食物与关切,
而这一切让公平洒满这个世界。
感谢您指引我们做应尽之事,
教导我们存慈悲之本心。
无论何时何地,您都与我们同在,
让我们成了更有爱心之人。

(丽贝卡·J.威斯顿)

Lesson 93

In rose time or in berry;
When ripe seeds fall or buds peep out;
When green the grass or white the rime;
There's something to be glad about.

(Lacy Larcom)

译文

无论是玫瑰飘香,还是浆果成熟;
无论是种子落地,还是花蕾绽放;
无论是草儿青青,还是白霜忽降;
美好的一刻总会悄然来临。

(拉西·拉科姆)

Lesson 94

I think of something.
It has two hands, but it has no feet.
One hand is short. One hand is long.
It has a face, but it has no head.
It can tell something, but cannot talk.
It can run, but cannot move.
Of what do I think?

(Answer : Clock)

译文

有个东西真有趣,
有两只手没脚丫,
双手一长又一短。
有张脸儿没脑袋,
不言不语会说话,
一动不动却能走。
猜猜这是什么呀?

(谜底:钟)